MW00443833

The
GREAT
HANDOFF

TERRY MUNDAY

dustjacket

Copyright ©2020 by Terry Mundy

©2020 Published by Dust Jacket Press
The Great Handoff: Christian organizations and the Intergenerational Transfer of Wealth / Terry Munday

ISBN: 978-1-947671-83-6

All rights reserved. This book or any portion thereof may not be reproduced or used in any manner whatsoever without the express written permission of the publisher except for the use of brief quotations in a book review.

Dust Jacket Press
P.O. Box 721243
Oklahoma City, OK 73172
www.dustjacket.com

Unless otherwise indicated, all Scripture quotations are taken from the Holy Bible, New International Version®, NIV® Copyright ©1973, 1978, 1984, 2011 by Biblica, Inc.® Used by permission. All rights reserved worldwide.

Scriptures taken from the New Living Translation. *Holy Bible*, New Living Translation, copyright © 1996, 2004, 2015 by Tyndale House Foundation. Used by permission of Tyndale House Publishers, Inc., Carol Stream, Illinois 60188. All rights reserved.

Scripture taken from the New King James Version®. Copyright © 1982 by Thomas Nelson. Used by permission. All rights reserved.

A special thank you to my daughter, Shelli Rowley and my granddaughters Hannah Rowley and Haleigh Rowley for their help in keyboarding the manuscript. Love you.

Cover and interior design by D. E. West, ZAQ Designs & Dust Jacket Creative Services

Printed in the United States of America

www.dustjacket.com

ENDORSEMENTS

"Terry Munday has enjoyed decades of remarkable success in raising financial resources for God's work because his passion for God's supply is exceeded only by the sincerity of his care for God's stewards. Those twin passions are evident in this book. Terry is desperately determined to help God's people see and seize the transformational potential of today's unprecedented intergenerational wealth transfer. Passionate appeal is accompanied by proven, practical advice that has the potential to change the trajectory and legacy of your stewardship now and for generations to come."

–Ralph Enlow, president of
The Association of Biblical Higher Education (ABHE)

"Terry's expertise and sense of mission allow him to paint a true picture of fundraising and what it can really mean to God's vision for the world."

– David Green, Founder of Hobby Lobby

"Terry's insight from three decades working as a fundraiser is rich in the humility, faith, and tenacity needed to make both your giving and receiving manifestations of God's love."

– Larry Maxwell,
President and Chairman of the Board, Century Funds, Inc.

"Terry Munday is THE EXPERT on teaching the foundational principles of fundraising. Our university has repeatedly asked him to train our staff in assisting people in achieving their charitable giving goals. Our world is witnessing the greatest transference of wealth to the next generation. In this book, Terry helps us to think through the most effective ways to do that so that Jesus' mission is effectively and strategically advanced."

–Dr. John Fozard,
President Mid America University, Oklahoma City, Oklahoma

"As a pediatric surgeon and former medical school faculty, I know that a diploma is just a fine paper without that next day of faithful practice. From that moment on, only a commitment to improvement will earn what a diploma declares. It is the only way to build a trust that allows people to let you guide them through the issues of life. Terry Munday is such a professional. I have had the opportunity to observe him as he served as Vice President of Advancement at Indiana Wesleyan University for the past nearly 20 years. His unique gift to meet people at their level and building financial wisdom and relationship on it makes him a friend and an outstanding fundraiser. In his book, The Great Handoff, Terry will demonstrate how charities can work to raise funds that promote their Christian causes."

–Darrell Hermann, M.D.

"What is our legacy? How do we transfer both our values and money to the next generation? How do we do the most good for our families and our communities? Terry Munday, former Vice President of Advancement at Indiana Wesleyan University, is uniquely qualified to help us think through our journey of generosity. He understands the unique perspectives of different generations; Millennials through Baby Boomers. He sensitively offers some new ideas, approaches and questions to ponder."

–Donald L. Palmer, Honey Creek Capital, LLC

"Terry has always understood life as stewardship. How do we invest our time, our wealth, our relationships, our passions for the greater good? This has given him an impactful career as a master fundraiser and a teacher of the linkage between our head and heart and what then happens with our bank account. Our beliefs and values should and must shape stewardship so that we are indeed investing in eternal things. THE GREAT HANDOFF makes this imperative clear."

–Curtis Smith, Chairman, Indiana Family Institute, an affiliate of Focus on the Family and the Alliance Defending Freedom.

"Terry changed the way our ministry asks for money, and as a result, our ministry is on solid ground. His wisdom in giving to the next generation has encouraged my husband and me to give the majority of our wealth to charity and leave the rest to help our children, not to enable them. Terry is an amazing Christian who lives out what he teaches. I am eternally grateful for his guidance.
–Nancy S Fitzgerald, Founder,
and Executive Director, Anchorsaway, Inc.

"Policy and procedure is the backbone of every organization. But unless they are realized in mission and motion, they are worthless. Terry Munday is a friend whose knowledge of fundraising policies and procedures has made him a stand-out in his profession. Add boldness, courage, and faith to the mix and you have the possibility of wide influence. Yet, his life has also been characterized by humility and kindness. To everyone responsible for raising monies for their organization, The Great Handoff will be an invaluable tool."
–Dick Anthony, Chairman Emeritus, Founder of IMMI.

"I loved my time working with you in the Advancement Office. It was always very clear to me that funding was your calling. You took so much pride in being able to move the mission of the University forward. Your heart showed in the way you gracefully handled each donor or in the way you acted crazy on the live TV auctions. I am a witness to your care for the students. I wouldn't have made it through college if it weren't for your personal commitment to me and to my success at IWU."
–Nathan Beals, former IWU student assistant.

DEDICATION

I am privileged to dedicate this book to my friend, Ross Hoffman. For 13 years, he served as my planned giving director, dedicating countless hours to traveling and sharing the cause of Indiana Wesleyan University and Christian higher education.

The owner of a successful insurance agency in Maine, Ross felt called to serve Christ in higher education. Driving him from the airport back to IWU for his interview, I knew within 20 minutes of conversation that he was the man for the job. And 20 years later in my tenure, I would still contend that hiring Ross was one of the best decisions I ever made.

He possessed a warm, thoughtful, and engaging spirit that everyone who met him immediately loved. And his spirit of kindness was particularly a magnet to our older donors. Ross was very instrumental in formulating several large estate gifts that made IWU a stronger university. Those gifts included the Art Hodson, Fred and Leveda Scripture, and David and Alene Blanchard estate gifts, to name a few. His gentle spirit and kindness to our donors endeared them to our university.

Ross and I spent many hours traveling for the University. Together we would visit donors, and many times be invited to stay in their homes. Later, when the University secured employee discounts from Marriott Hotels, we would share a room to save costs. I recall several nights when we were still traveling at 10:00 o'clock in the evening, Ross would say, "Munday you're killing me, I need to get these contacts out!" But the next morning, he was ready to hit the road.

The love Ross had for retirement-age people became apparent when he planned and carried out our annual *Chaparral* travel tours. For 18 years, our guests had four days of sightseeing, fellowship, and relaxation while Ross accommodated their every need. Traveling to such places as Charleston, Savannah, Washington D.C., Lancaster, or Williamsburg, the tours became annual vacation trips for many. At times, over 250 travelers in one trip would enjoy the sights and the fellowship of the *Chaparrals*. And thanks to Ross' efforts, those trips generated scholarship money for IWU students. Many of the attendees invited him to their homes and made substantial contributions. Relationships matter and Ross was a master of developing them.

I'll never forget the day I received that telephone call. I was at a local restaurant, watching a TV stream of a professional baseball game, with one of our IWU alumni, Brandon Beachy, pitching. The caller said Ross had been involved in an accident at his home and was being transported to Marion General Hospital. I rushed to the hospital and was one of the first to arrive, but within minutes more than 25-30 friends also arrived to pray and support the family. We soon heard the dreaded news that Ross had passed. We mourned the loss, but even there we celebrated his life and the joy he must have known to meet his Savior.

As I wrote this book about the importance of planned giving, I thought it only appropriate to recognize the importance of Ross Hoffman to the legacy of Indiana Wesleyan University, and of his importance in my life. I'm so thankful to be one of so many who called him a best friend.

To his wife, Karen, and children, Logan and Jolee, I say thank you for carrying on his rich legacy. He was so proud of you. And your continued service to the Lord would make him even prouder. Only eternity will tell of the many lives Ross Hoffman impacted for the Kingdom with his steadfast faith, excellent service, loving spirit, caring words, and kind deeds.

Terry Munday

CONTENTS

FOREWORD

Terry Munday is a friend with a generous heart and a Christlike mission. From his faith, wisdom, and stewardship, he has committed his life to help people around the world develop biblically sound principles for raising, managing, and distributing resources God has provided for them. A successful businessman and retired Vice President for University Advancement at Indiana Wesleyan University, Terry Munday has raised millions of dollars for Christian organizations and institutions. Always willing to pay it forward, he has used his vast experience to benefit other fundraisers in their ventures. You might say he is a "Fundraiser's Fundraiser."

His insights are invaluable for this time when the greatest transfer of wealth in history is already in motion. It's called the Great Wealth Transfer, and it will see an intergenerational transfer that could exceed $41 trillion by 2050. Terry is tirelessly informing Christian organizations to take advantage of it as he speaks in seminars and conferences across the nation. As he has learned from proven leaders in his profession, you can learn from his own leadership. Your life and organization will be the richer for it.

Terry's experience as a teacher, coach, and school administrator will be obvious as he leads you through this practical book. You will learn biblical principles about the stewardship of wealth, and how it applies to fundraising. And you will see how those principles relate to the values and giving patterns of donors in each generation. You will also learn how to target, cultivate, and make the all-important "Ask" for donor contributions.

His faith in Jesus Christ is obvious and real. It has been forged in a lifetime of trusting God. And for Terry and his wife Linda, that trust was proven in surviving the tragic death of their son, Michael, a Marine Corps veteran who committed suicide after suffering from Post-Traumatic Stress Syndrome. They have been quick to share what they experienced of God's grace and wisdom during that time. It was a tragedy that God turned to a ministry, further extending their impact by participating in programs that honor and assist Armed Forces veterans and their families.

The Great Handoff: Christian Organizations and the Intergenerational Transfer of Wealth is a book that has been tested in the changing climates of the economy and will prove to be a blessing to everyone responsible for organizational fundraising. I've seen the results of Terry Munday's tireless work for Christian institutions in the lives of students, including my grandchild. My thanks to Terry for his friendship and for continuing to inspire others with his love for the Lord and the work of God's kingdom on earth.

David Green,
Founder, Hobby Lobby

INTRODUCTION

It was the final race of the day. A 800-meter relay race and the outcome would mean the difference between winning or losing the track meet. Four runners would run two laps around the 400-meter track. I knew my team was feeling the pressure of the race—along with the crowd of fans and family watching them. The first three runners had completed their run, and the final runner, the anchor runner, was about to receive the baton. The handoff would be crucial. It's made blindly, the runner with the baton reaches toward the next runner, in this case, the final runner.

Standing near the finish line, I nervously anticipated the exchange, somewhat assured that our fastest runner would be getting the handoff. Then, suddenly, the disqualification flag went up! DISQUALIFIED! The runner hadn't received the handoff within the 20-meter exchange zone. He had been running a great race, and now this! The agony of defeat was etched in his face. He heard the cheers turn to an aching silence. He saw the drooped heads of his teammates. He watched as the winning team jubilantly celebrated the win. As the track coach, my heart ached more for the runner than for the loss. He would likely remember that failed handoff for the rest of his life.

PASSING THE BATON

This book is about the handoff, a great handoff of wealth that could benefit every Christian organization. Specifically, we are at the leading edge of the largest intergenerational transfer of wealth in world history. It's estimated that in the next 30 years, over 40 trillion dollars will be passed from one generation to the next. Forty trillion dollars by 2050! Finance professionals estimate that 7% of that wealth transfer will go to nonprofits. Others feel that charitable giving could be as much as $27 trillion if the economy continues to grow at 2% and $40 trillion if the economic growth rate is 3%. We know that nearly 50% of Americans give nothing to charity while 25% of all Americans give more than $500. The 25% of donors represent an immediate opportunity for identifying, contacting, cultivating, and asking for major donations.

THERE IS AN URGENCY

I am not an enthusiast of theories that teach an end-time "bonus" from the wealth of the unrighteous. Nor am I suggesting that anyone has an insider view of God's final redemption apart from what He has already revealed in His Word, the Bible. I am simply saying that Christian organizations need to be asking, "How can my charity profit from the intergenerational transfer of wealth?" The need to be proactive is a given! Only 22% of Americans over the age of 30 reports having been asked for a planned gift. Generations that will inherit the wealth are probably more interested in making gifts before death, and that is where planned giving can have a major impact. It will not only generate an investment return but also have a positive effect on your organization. Since the ultra-wealthy are in control of a large portion of transferable wealth, they will have the greatest effect on charitable giving. The extremely-wealthy, who still value not spoiling their children or destroying their incentive to work hard, will provide their children with a major gift—but the remainder of their wealth will go to charity. And they will want to see an immediate impact from their giving.

RELATIONSHIPS ARE IMPORTANT

I contend that charities need to overcome their fear that planned giving will require an attorney on staff or a certified planned giving specialist. Granted, those professionals will be needed as the process with the individual unfolds. But the same personal relationship that fundraisers use during the annual fund drive can be transferred to the process of planned giving. The process is aided by a personal touch and includes *identifying* the donor, *cultivating* a relationship with the donor, and *asking* the donor for a specific donation.

The estimated numbers before us are staggering:

- $12 trillion in assets has already changed hands in the form of inheritance from the Silent Generation (born 1928-1945) to Baby Boomers (born 1946-1964).

- Between 2011 and 2048, Baby Boomers are expected to transfer another $30 to $41 trillion to Generation X (born 1964 -1980) and Millennials (born 1980-1996).

- $59 trillion is the amount projected to change hands if we expand this time frame from 2007 to 2061, with at least $39 trillion going to heirs,

It can't be business as usual or we will continue to reap small dividends for our efforts. For example, we must increase our efforts with the Baby Boomer generation. In 2018, CNBC reported that Baby Boomers are the wealthiest generation in history and will turn over $68 trillion over the next 25 years. We will need to spend a disproportionate amount of our time working with this group. Someone who has been loyal and consistent in giving over the years deserves a greater commitment of our time. In the spirit of the 80/20 Pareto Rule, we must remember that 10% of the people will give 90% of the money. In addition, we need to make certain our donors are familiar with our mission and the work that is being done by our charity to accomplish it. We cannot assume that our donors have knowledge of our efforts. The donor needs to know the lives we are touching and the differences we are making in their lives and in the world. And stories are a great way to convey that mission.

IMPACTING SOCIETY

Everyone wants to be bigger than themselves. And they can leave a legacy by leaving a planned gift or major gift to their favorite charity. We must make a stronger appeal for legacy opportunities in our charitable giving. Estate planning is at 5% among Americans and about 70% of Americans do not yet have a will, and only 15% have provided for charitable causes. Those of us in the not-for-profit sector especially have a great deal of work to do—and we need to get started, working with our donor bases in the area of planned giving. We have great potential in realizing charitable gifts. There are many untapped resources, and many who are already giving can increase their level of giving. The problem in America is that we have a few people giving a lot and many giving nothing or far too little. The call should be for all people to give if we are going to impact society. And impact it, we must. The organizations and institutions we serve are fortresses that are being used to stem the tide of humanism that is threatening to destroy our values and beliefs. We are not just fundraisers; we are trustees of the blessings God has passed to us in the greatest handoff of all.

The Great Handoff: Christian Organizations and the Intergenerational Transfer of Wealth is my gift to you, my fellow professionals. In four important areas I will share what I have learned about:

- The Biblical Landscape of Wealth

- The Donor Base

- The Great Wealth Transfer

- The "Ask," Systems and Strategies of Fundraising.

My prayer is that you will learn from these biblical and practical principles and that you will implement them with even greater application in the greatest cause of all: God's kingdom in heaven and on earth.

Terry Munday, 2020

"God dwells in His creation and is everywhere
indivisibly present in all His works."
– A. W. Tozer

CHAPTER 1

The Fundamentals of Ownership and Stewardship

At the very core of the Great Handoff is the question: "Whose wealth is it? Yours, mine, or His?" Parents of toddlers know what it is to deal with the "Mines!" When it comes to possessions, "MINE!" seems to be the natural reaction and "Share" the learned reaction.

A story by Greg Laurie proves the "mines" aren't limited to toddlers. "GET OUT OF THE CAR! I HAVE A GUN AND I KNOW HOW TO USE IT!" an elderly lady yelled as she carried a bag of groceries back to her car and saw four strangers sitting in it. Fortunately, she carried a registered handgun to deal with such a threat. Dropping the groceries, she reached into her purse and pulled out the gun. Pointing it at the intruders, she screamed, "OUT OF THE CAR! RIGHT NOW! The driver and three passengers quickly got out of the car and started running with their hands up.

Still shaking, the lady put her groceries in the passenger seat and got behind the wheel. But when she tried to put her key in the ignition, it wouldn't fit. A quick glance through the window solved the problem. A few parking spaces away was a car that looked just like hers—AND WAS HER'S. Sheepishly retrieving her grocery bag, she looked to see if anyone saw the mistake and got into her car. She drove to the police station and made her confession to the desk sergeant. He laughed and turned to the people at the other end of the counter, "Is this the old lady with a gun that hijacked your car?" They had overheard her confession and answered through their laughter, "That's her!" And the case was closed.

It is human to defend what we think is ours. Over the years, I have heard people share stories of how they were cheated out of an inheritance by a family member who claimed what they thought was theirs. But does the "what's mine is mine" philosophy really hold up? The Bible says "The earth is the LORD's, and everything in it. The world and all its people belong to him" (Psalm 24:1). He built it from nothing and graced it with everything! We are steward/managers of God's blessings and are called to give a spiritual account of their use. God is the Source. James 1:17, "Every good and perfect gift is from above, coming down from the Father of the heavenly lights." Whatever we have comes from His holy supply.

GOD'S ECONOMY

Out of His riches and goodness, God established an economy that provides resources and skills for us to survive and thrive. Genesis 2:8-9, "Now the Lord God had planted a garden in the east, in Eden; and there he put the man he had formed. The Lord God made all kinds of trees grow out of the ground—trees that were pleasing to the eye and good for food." He also provided the capacity to understand the natural world so they could make use of it. Genesis 2:15, "The Lord God took the man and put him in the Garden of Eden to work it and take care of it." God's blessings sustain us—such as talent and health for our work, opportunities to be educated, and a government with a rule of law. Those advantages are to be used to acknowledge His ownership, glorify Him, and bring honor to His name. But an estimated 1.4 billion people in the world live in extreme poverty. An additional 1.1 billion live at a subsistence level, i.e., they are only one crisis away from disaster. This is not the way God intended it in the beginning. It is the way His created people chose when they decided to go their own way.

Though we are not born on a level playing field, all of us who were born in America should be grateful for our place of birth. There are 8.6 million households with a net worth of at least $1 million, 1 million households with a net worth of $5 million, and over 100,000 households with a net of $25 million in the US. We get a head start on others—maybe to an unfair advantage. According to the United Nations, nearly half of the world's population earns less than $2 per day. The poorest person in the US is in the highest 5% of wage earners in the world. I believe that God has planted wisdom and skills in every person on earth that can help to reverse their extreme condition—if they will acknowledge His ownership and practice the principles of His Word. The Bible is realistic about dealing with poverty and wealth. It does not connect provisions (or their lack) with a certain cause, it just commands those who have plenty to care for those who lack. His promises are always linked with our responses. And our spiritual wholeness comes through our obedience—including in our giving.

> *"A wise man should have money in his head, not in his heart."*
> – Jonathan Swift

David Kotter, a senior research fellow for the Institute for Faith, Work and Economics, defines wealth as a "suitable accumulation of resources and possessions of value" [food, clothing, and protection]. The definition of basic needs has changed in our society. Kotter draws a distinction between wealth and riches. They are not interchangeable. Spiritually, the difference is in the attitude of the heart. Kotter notes that riches correspond with a self-indulgent heart and wealth with being stewards of God's gifts and their management to honor God.[1] When we die, everything we have stays behind—that new car in the garage; that 4-bedroom, 3-bath home; that Hart Schaffner & Marx suit we wear; and even those Johnston & Murphy shoes on our feet. We are stewards, not owners. Our job is to be faithful to Him with the things He has entrusted to us.

When I started teaching in 1970, I signed a contract for $6,000 per year. That was a great increase over my paycheck for that part-time job I had at Greeno's Heating while finishing college, and certainly, more than I earned baling hay for the neighbor in my teen years. My point is that our stewardship duties start at lower levels and continue at each subsequent level for our working life. So, what is our responsibility based on what God has given to us? How much should we save, spend or give? Being a Christian steward means giving up ownership of the products we purchase, no matter their quality. Though we have been blessed with nice things, it does not mean that we prize them more. Everything we have is on loan from the One who owns it all.

THE BIBLE AND WEALTH

The Apostle Paul asked first-century Christians, "What do you have that you did not receive from God?" (1 Corinthians 4:7). That's a good question to ask of everyone, and the answer is "Nothing!" At 70 1/2 years of age, I knew I would need to take 3-4% of my IRA's Required Minimum Distribution (RMD) out of our retirement funds or pay a penalty. By acknowledging God's ownership and provision, it was an easy decision to give monies generated to charity. Matthew 10:8, "Freely you have received, freely give." The Bible does not say that wealth is an indication of God's favor, or that poverty is an indication of His punishment. It says, "He causes his sun to rise on the evil and the good and sends rain on the righteous and the unrighteous" (Matthew 5:45). God provides the land, puts vision and skill in the people, and then allows them a free will to make wise or foolish decisions that will result in a boom or bust. But there's no written guarantee, despite those who teach a "health and wealth" message. The fact is, many wealthy people mentioned in the Bible did not prosper because of their righteousness, they prospered in their wickedness—by using selfish human methods.

Christians are called to be responsible spenders. For example, by our stewardship/management of God's resources, we learn to be content with what we have and to practice generosity at the same time. We need to be able to determine when enough is enough as it relates to money. Living richly means figuring out what to spend your time, money, and energy on. You must prioritize. I have tried to practice that in my home. TIME magazine contributing author, Mary Eberstadt, asserts, "The fortunes of religion rise or fall with the state of the family." The breakdown of the family is one large culprit in this process. Adult role models have not been consistent in living out their faith.

> *"The greatest use of money is to spend it on something that will outlast it."*
> – William James

Teaching children to spend responsibly begins early—and often insignificantly. I have always enjoyed taking my family out to eat. But they all knew I aligned with the disclaimer, "beverages not included." I saw that policy as a way to teach my children delayed gratification. By not ordering soft drinks with the meal, I tried to teach my children how to prioritize and make good decisions. Those beverages that cost pennies to make cost dollars for our family to drink. "Too much, too soon" is a philosophy that many parents or grandparents may be guilty of in spoiling their family members—and it's not limited to adding a soft drink to a burger order. Research by Ameriprise Financial Study revealed that two-thirds of Baby Boomers help with college loan payments, more than half help family members buy a new car, and one-third assist their adult children with routine expenses.

God's creation has a factory-installed obligation to give back. Planets provide direction and light. Oceans water the earth. Trees and flowers sow seeds to the wind. Plants furnish oxygen. Clouds protect from scorching. People are not excluded. What they give to the planet replenishes it and cares for it—and bring honor to their Creator.

People also have an opportunity to give back their Creator. He certainly doesn't need the money—His riches are limitless. But from His love and wisdom, He gave the law of the tithe (10% of our income) as a way for us to,

- Acknowledge His ownership.
- Practice budgeted spending.
- Support the advancement of His kingdom on earth.

It is an equitable and practical way to "practice our faith." J. L. Kraft, founder of the Kraft business empire said, "The only investments I ever made that have paid constantly increasing dividends are those I have given to the Lord's work." I venture to say we all could give more. We may not have great wealth, but we still have a responsibility to give generously out of what we do have. I have heard the excuses for not giving, like, "I'm not sure how the charity will spend the money" or "I can't afford to give money so I give my time" or "I work for a company that uses their profit for charity, so I am part of their giving." I have reminded board members that if they give "time" they are a volunteer, and if they give money, they are donors, but they are expected to do both. Light bills can't be paid with "time."

I once had a colleague who told me he wasn't experiencing joy in his Christian faith. During our conversation, he revealed that he hadn't been able to pay his tithe. Immediately I knew one of the reasons why he lacked joy. Joy isn't from what we have, it is from what we give in alignment with God and His Word. He wasn't being responsible for the blessings God had given him. I suggested to him that the tithe is a reasonable request and he needed to cut expenditures in the household in order to be able to pay (not "give") his tithe. Thankfully, he later reported that he and the family had adjusted to the cut and had started a tithing plan. He said the joy he now felt made him wish he had started tithing many years ago. Giving won't become easier as the paycheck gets larger; giving starts with what we have right now.

DISCERNMENT IN GIVING

The development of our Christian faith is dependent on our listening to the leadership of the Holy Spirit—including in our giving. Many people are overwhelmed by the number of giving requests. During the last three months of the year, October through December, 30-40% of all gifts to nonprofits are received. For that reason, most of us are inundated with requests from community nonprofits, our churches, and other institutions during that time. I've been asked how I determine what charities are most in need. I think it is important to prayerfully consider the requests and make the decision based on God's leadership through your resources. First, which organizations are truly assisting those less fortunate? And second, does the charity have an open and honest approach to its expenditures? It is not unreasonable to review the charity's budget to make certain the dollars are being expended in the way it claims. And it's not unreasonable to ask how much of its expenditures are spent on administration. The income/distribution ratio in some charities can be alarming. The extra research can be invaluable in choosing your charities. Generosity isn't the source of our faith; it is the evidence. And the Scriptures tell us to pass that faith—and that evidence—along to our children and their families.

When I ask major donors, "Who taught you to give?" they invariably refer to the example of their parents. I have many memories of my parents living by the principle of putting the needs of others before their own. If my mother heard of a family in need, she would find some way to help, whether it be items from the garden or clothes that my siblings or I had outgrown. With the help of her Singer sewing machine, she could transform an unused garment into something valued by someone else.

During my teenage years, our family made regular visits to the Barberton, Ohio Rescue Mission. Each time we loaded the car with food and clothing which provided the men and women with assistance. Since the residents of the mission were required to attend the nightly services, we were always interested to see how many of the clothing items would be worn to that service. And without fail, there were items we had donated being worn by the Mission's residents—Dad's suit coat, one of my shirts, or a dress that Mom had altered. Little did I know that Mom and Dad were teaching my sisters and me the value of money management and giving.

Also, as a child, I received payment for my work or chores. And my parents reminded me of my obligation to pay my tithe (10%) from my earnings into the "storehouse"—the local church. I am not certain how many dollars Mom and Dad put into the offering plate, but I knew it was at the very least, their tithe. During my years as a youth sponsor, my youth pastor used to teach the principles of giving by handing each student a yellow cup labeled "Isaiah 6 Project." Students were told to place the cup in an area near where they laid their change each night, and any change they accumulated was to be brought back to the group as an offering. It was surprising to see how much money was collected by 150 students through this method of giving. To this day, over 30 years later, I have that yellow cup on my dresser to catch my extra coins.

SPIRITUAL FORMATION

Our giving is part of our spiritual formation. I have mentioned before the importance of modeling giving to our children and peers. Interestingly, in this digital age, researchers have determined that the use of online giving may be a deterrent to generations giving in the future. Why? Because they fail to witness the act of their parent's giving. In many cases that public display may be the only act of giving our children will see. Giving is an act of worship, so in the truest sense, then, our church doesn't "take" our offering, it "receives" it in recognition of our spiritual growth. Obedience is the foundation. Malachi 3:10a, "Bring the whole tithe into the storehouse, that there may be food in my house" is God's promise. And He adds, "'Test me in this,' says the Lord Almighty, and see if I will not throw open the floodgates of heaven and pour out so much blessing that there will not be room enough to store it" (Malachi 3:10b). We will never win a giving contest with God. Talking about giving with David Green in Oklahoma City one day, he said something that I felt was profound, "We hear people saying all the time that you can't out-give God, so I ask them, 'Have you ever tried?'"

GIVING GIVES BACK

Earthly institutions promise both tiny percentage-point returns and often exaggerated returns when we make an investment. But Heaven throws its floodgates open and "pours out a blessing" when we obey God's Word.

Jesus affirmed, "Give, and it will be given to you. A good measure, pressed down, shaken together and running over, will be poured into your lap" (Luke 6:38). The very exercise of giving is not only good for you, but it is also good for everyone who observes it. Remember the Bible story of Jesus watching as the widow gave her temple offering of two small coins. He remarked, "Truly I tell you this poor widow has put more into the treasury than all the others. They all gave out of their wealth; but she, out of her poverty, put in everything—all she had to live on" (Mark 12:43). It wasn't just about the amount; it was about obedient sacrifice.

Faith always needs a giving outlet to grow. I have seen that in my own life and in the life of my friends. About four years ago, we started a school called Kinwell Academy to help students who have dropped out of high school and are seeking a chance to achieve a high school diploma. Currently, we have about 40 students in that school. A good friend, Van Gurley, whom I have known for about 25 years, asked me what I was doing in my retirement. I shared about the school. Van immediately said, "I have an interest in that kind of thing. Send me some information." I did, and about a week later I received a check for the school for $7,000. It wasn't a usual "Ask," it was a heartfelt response from someone who heard the story and wanted to support young people. God's goodness to us is best acknowledged by our service to others in His name.

> *"God gives, but man must open his hand."*
> – German Proverb

WEALTH AND THE BIBLE

The Bible says wealth is a gift from God to be used in service to Him and to others. You shall remember the Lord your God, for it is he who gives you the power to get wealth" (Deuteronomy 8:18). The dictionary says wealth is an abundance of possessions or resources. Others may say it is a prosperity that brings evident happiness. And yet we have hundreds of stories about the failure of wealth to bring true happiness. In fact, modern history proves that sudden wealth can bring gradual unhappiness. Lottery winners are a case in point. One study said, "Nearly one-third of U.S. lottery winners declare bankruptcy, often within just a few years of their big win… After sizable tax obligations, lavish spending decisions and prior monetary commitments…winning the lotto is often more of a curse than a blessing." [2] That pairs with the pain brought by those who exploit others for money, including force, corruption, theft, and such things as Ponzi schemes. It proves the biblical truth that "The love of money is the root of all kinds of evil. And some people, craving money, have wandered from the true faith and pierced themselves with many sorrows" (1 Timothy 6:10, NLT).

In a biblical context, I would describe wealth as spiritual, relational, and material blessings from God in response to obeying His laws of money management and giving. Author and pastor, Greg Laurie, wrote, "When Jesus said, 'Do not lay up for yourselves treasures on earth'(Matthew 6:19), the term 'lay-up' did not simply speak of having possessions, but of your possessions having you. "Lay up" could be better translated "hoard" or "stockpile." Jesus was not saying it is wrong to have things. He was warning against becoming materialistic—letting things become more important than God." [3]

WEALTHY AND WISE

Studying wealth and riches in history is a study of "rich" families, passing their wealth along from generation to generation. That is much different from the temporary wealth of dot-com entrepreneurs whose fortunes blossomed and wilted, professional athletes whose multi-million dollar signing bonuses crumbled into a spot on the trading block, or casino winners who can win and lose a fortune in the same evening. Wealthy people have knowledge that enables them to *achieve* wealth while rich people *have* money. The wealthy can withstand the ups and downs of the market. Solomon asked God for wisdom and that in turn created his wealth. I think wisdom can be divided in two ways: 1. That which comes with education and practice, and, 2. That which comes from spiritual disciplines.

Long before I achieved university degrees, I "went to school" in my father's business and gained wisdom through *education and practice*. Dad owned a construction business and I was expected to work on roofing, plumbing, heating, and overall construction and renovating. As a result, I acquired a knowledge of construction that I used when I purchased and remodeled rental homes that became a source of income and an opportunity to grow retirement money for my family.

Spiritual wisdom is ongoing and comes through my faith and the disciplines of holy living. The Bible is an eternally relevant manual—a library filled with practical insights that make life livable. The disciplined practice of prayer and Bible study opened my heart and mind to the Holy Spirit-inspired writings of the Scriptures. Bible instruction and Spirit-led counsel have directed my decisions and served as my moral and ethical compass through life.

In my association with people who are considered wealthy, I have noticed several characteristics.

- Wealthy people are value creators and do more than what is expected. They choose to redeem their time in a constructive manner.

- The wealthy learn from others, adopting proven methods for financial growth. Many people live paycheck to paycheck and spend their money on luxury items, but wealthy people focus on spending their money on investment opportunities that will cause their money to grow.

- The wealthy are frugal. They save more than they consume.

- The wealthy spend time planning. They spend money selectively and are not caught in the "Keeping up with the Joneses" cycle.

- The wealthy operate under the premise that adult children who receive less will be motivated to achieve more on their own merits.

- The wealthy care for their own. 80% of millionaires care for first-generation millionaires.

DANGEROUSLY WEALTHY

Old Testament prophets like Amos, Micah, and Jeremiah taught that our worship is meaningless if we are accumulating wealth through the exploitation of others. Amos said judgment was coming on the people of Israel in his day because they "sell the righteousness for silver and the needy for a pair of sandals." Solomon, the Old Testament wisdom writer prayed, "Give me neither poverty nor riches; feed me with the food that I need, or I shall be full, and deny you and say 'Who is the Lord' or I shall be poor, and steal, and profane the name of my God (Proverbs 30:8-9).

Charles Schwab said for Americans to live "comfortably" they would need $1.4 million, and to live a life of "luxury (wealthy)" they would need $2.4 million. But most Americans would probably consider "comfortable living" as being able to meet housing and transportation expenses—and their monthly cable and streaming video services. Definitions of "wealth" are variables defined by lifestyles. Even "wealthy" is a matter of interpretation—and often has as many pitfalls as premiums.

"There are over 2300 references to money and possessions in the Word of God."
— Elmer Towns

Wealth can cause pride and arrogance. The problem isn't gain; the problem is greed. Wealth is not neutral. It is aggressive and insatiable. When do we have enough? If we have $100,000, we want $500,000. If we have $500,000, we want $1 million, and on and on. Ezekiel the prophet warned a king of Israel, "By your great wisdom in trade you have increased your wealth, and your heart has become proud in your wealth" (Ezekiel 28:15). Jesus said, "It is easier for a camel to go through the eye of a needle than for someone who is rich to enter the kingdom of God" (Matthew 19:23-24). Of course, the amount of money one has in the bank doesn't determine whether they can be a Christian. What determines a Christian (Christ-follower) is WHO or WHAT lives and rules in that person's heart. The Bible says those who receive Christ, who believe in His name, "He gave the right to become children of God" (John 1:12).

Wealth can be very good or very destructive. The more wealth one has the greater the risk. As early as 1929, Floyd Allen, an executive with General Motors, put it bluntly, "Advertising is the business of making people dissatisfied with what they have in favor of something better." You will never hear advertisers say, "you don't need anything." In our materialistic society, we are conditioned to always want more.

Wealth may cause us to have less empathy and compassion. A UC Berkeley study found that at a crosswalk, drivers of luxury cars were 4-times less likely than those in less expensive vehicles to stop and allow pedestrians the right of way.

Wealth may make us vulnerable to disorders. Wealthier children seem to be more prone to anxiety, depression, eating disorders, cheating and stealing than lower-income children. Career obligations cause wealthy families to have less family time which impacts emotional stability. Studies have found that affluent children are more vulnerable to substance abuse issues. The rich outdrink the poor by more than 27%.

Wealth often causes more stress. Most people who have plenty (or more) develop insidious stress. They worry. Having arrived makes them anxious that they might lose some of their stuff. The fear of not having enough drives some to overwork. That is one reason members of the Baby Boomer generation are known for their "workaholicism." They work to provide the latest and greatest for their children and grandchildren. Baby Boomers, in particular, are known for buying 80% of online sales—much, if not even most of it for gadgets. But what our children need is more of mom and dad's time and attention. Others wonder if they'll have enough money to sustain them throughout their life. So, they spend time chasing the almighty dollar at the cost of serving God and others. And they buy the latest in material possessions at the expense of developing rich and meaningful relationships.

FOR EXAMPLE

I have great admiration for my son-in-law, who always has time for his children—my grandkids. Whether playing ball, tossing the Frisbee, or playing board games, he's there. And music concerts, tennis matches, etc., are always on his calendar. He is busy, but not too busy to be an on-site dad to his children. So, I'm never too busy to lend him a hand in his efforts—including having my tree trimmer cut logs to fit the woodstove he uses to heat his home during the winter. That is the least I can do to help him extend the time he spends with my grandchildren.

Max Jukes lived in New York. He did not believe in Christ or in Christian training. He refused to take his children to church, even when they asked to go. Of his 1,026 descendants, 300 were imprisoned—27 as murderers and 190 as prostitutes. In addition, 509 family members were alcoholics or drug addicts. Thus far, his family has reportedly cost the state hundreds of thousands of dollars. And as far as we know, Max Jukes' family has made no worthy contributions to their society. His habit of not taking the time to develop a values system is sadly evident in his legacy.

By contrast, Jonathan Edwards lived in the same state, at the same time as Jukes. He loved the Lord and saw to it that his children were in church every Sunday, where he served the Lord to the best of his ability. Among his 929 descendants were 430 ministers, 314 military veterans, 75 authors, 86 college professors, 13 university presidents, 7 congressmen, 3 governors, and a Vice President of the United States. His family contributed immeasurably to the life of plenty in the US today.

The biographer of Frederick Meijer, the billionaire founder of the Meijer supermarket chain, said, Meijer didn't think of his charitable giving as unusual generosity, he thought of it as trying to create a complete life for himself, his family, and his community… he says 'If we enjoy the past, then we ought to contribute to the future.' [4] Peter Singer wrote in the *New York Times* about the enormous wealth of several well-known Americans and the lesser-known needs of people in other countries. "In the same world in which more than a billion people live at a level of affluence never previously known, roughly a billion other people struggle to survive on the purchasing power equivalent of less than one US dollar per day." He tells of a man named Zell Kravinsky, who donated nearly his entire $45 million estate to health-related charities. But when he learned that thousands of people with kidney failure die each year while waiting for a donor's kidney, Kravinsky called a hospital and arranged to donate one of his kidneys to a complete stranger. [5]

I wonder how many of us view wealth in terms of eternity versus living the 70-90 years on this earth. We have the responsibility to give our best. We should be giving to expand the impact Christ can have on others. Recently I was involved in a major gift campaign at a church. The attempt was to raise 2.7 million to build additional facilities for youth that would expand Christ's kingdom in future generations. The donors knew that their gifts would provide the gospel message to young people and make Christ known for many years to come. Over the years I have met individuals who question whether tithing their income (10%) is really necessary. I say it is—and I might add it seems to be the minimum. Gordon McDowell says, "Generous giving starts when it hurts to give. When one moves in the direction of poverty in order to make someone else rich."

I've said that hard work was once the reason for financial success, but now I believe hard work AND rich parents is a plus! But, none of us can guarantee the direction our children will take, we can only provide a values system that is biblically based and focused on their spiritual development. The rest is up to the Lord—and their spiritual choices. But in so doing, we leave them a positive and purposeful legacy.

I've always admired the legendary UCLA basketball coach, John Wooden, called the "Wizard of Westwood." His teams won 10 NCAA national championships and built one of the greatest basketball dynasties in history. But more than his coaching skills, I admired his work ethic, his positive spirit, and most of all his faith. I met him in Lexington, Kentucky at the Marriott hotel. Knowing his humble Indiana roots, I asked him if he would autograph a basketball that would be auctioned at the annual Jack Colescott golf outing at IWU. He graciously obliged, I think out of his desire to see a Christian university excel. I later sent two additional basketballs and asked for his signature; he responded by signing and sending a note that wished us well in our endeavors.

Each time I reached out to him after that meeting, he went beyond the call of duty to respond. I am grateful for men of his reputation who are uncompromising in their core values and set a high standard of Christian living. Throughout his fabled career, he carried a card his father had given to him in the eighth grade. Wooden's father said as he handed it to him,

"Try to live up to this." On the card were seven principles that shaped his life and career:

1. Be true to yourself.

2. Help others.

3. Make friendship a fine art.

4. Drink deeply from good books, especially the Bible.

5. Make each day your masterpiece.

6. Build a shelter against a rainy day by the life you live.

7. Give thanks for your blessings and pray for guidance every day.

Wisdom wise, it was a Great Handoff. And an example to all of us who see the need to pass our value system along to others.

I am convinced that as fundraisers and other financial professionals, we often ask our donors for gifts that will make us look good in the eyes of our leaders. But if we are asking for a Christian cause, we'd better be asking in order to advance the kingdom of God and not our own position. Paul the Apostle said, "Christ who was rich choose to become poor so that you might become spiritually rich." What a great transfer of wealth. And what a great example for us! Spiritual riches versus one's financial worth. Our sense of worth must not come from the number of toys we accumulate, the square footage in our house, or our membership in the country club.

I have learned that money is only one part of our success or wealth. After 50 years of marriage, raising four children, running a house rental operation, and serving as a university fundraiser, I find that the truest measure of wealth is found in things that do not have price tags. And I've found that the truest joy is found in living in a way that pleases God and is aligned with His Word. It is a priority that serves as my primary focus—and envelopes my relationship with family and friends. *I am wealthy in family life.* I admit that I have not always been the best at balancing work and family time, but I am thankful for a wife who helped me balance the deficit. *I am wealthy in friendships.* The formal and informal times of being with friends have enriched my thinking and expanded my vision. *I am wealthy in opportunity.* God has given me skills and wisdom to make wise financial choices and to make frugal decisions that provide for my family and generate retirement funds.

I regret that our culture is consumed with money, that its eyes monitor accumulations, bank accounts, or stocks and bonds. I regret that we have little time to study God's Word and allow Him to direct our decision making. Jesus taught about a "rich young ruler" who went away with sadness. He had asked the right question, asked the right person, got the right answer, but he made the wrong decision. As fundraisers, we have a responsibility to help people with the wrong attitudes toward wealth to realize their lack of priority and repent in sorrow. The late pastor and author, Robert Schuller, said it right, "God gives to us what He knows will flow through us."

"Abraham gave everything he owned to his son Isaac."
– Genesis 25:5, NLT

CHAPTER 2

Wealth Transfer in Bible Times

The intergenerational transfer of wealth isn't a new emphasis. It's as old as the ark and as new as a luxury cruise ship. If you think that, since the Bible was written so long ago and represented such a different economy, is not relevant in today's world, you should think again. The eternally relevant Word of God is not silent about wealth. Greg Laurie, wrote, "15-percent of everything Jesus ever taught was on the topic of money and possessions—more than His teachings on heaven and hell combined."[6]

MONEY MANAGEMENT

With thanks to best-selling author and financial planner, Ron Blue, a pioneer in writings about Christian money management, I use his outline from the chapter on the "Four Biblical Principles of Money Management," in his book, *Master Your Money*.[7] It is based on Jesus' parable of the talents (Matthew 25) and features biblical principles for wealth transfer in Bible times. Though the parable is from the New Testament, its root teaching covers the entirety of Bible teaching on the subject.

1. GOD OWNS IT ALL

Matthew 25:14, [The kingdom of heaven] "will be like a man going on a journey, who called his servants and entrusted his wealth to them." Note, God (the owner), entrusts HIS WEALTH to HIS servants. We are His servants—the steward/managers of the wealth He has entrusted to us. In Bible times, the devout acknowledged that everything they had or that surrounded them belonged to God. They lived by the reminder God gave to their leader, Moses.

> The Lord your God will soon bring you into the land he swore to give you when He made a vow to your ancestors Abraham, Isaac, and Jacob. It is a land with large, prosperous cities that you did not build. The houses will be richly stocked with goods you did not produce. You will draw water from cisterns you did not dig, and you will eat from vineyards and olive trees you did not plant. When you have eaten your fill in this land, be careful not to forget the Lord, who rescued you from slavery in the land of Egypt. – Deuteronomy 6:10-12, NLT

Philosopher and theologian, William A. Dembski, wrote, "Who's right, the ancients or the moderns? My own view is that the ancients got it right. An act of creation is always a divine gift and cannot be reduced to purely naturalistic categories. To be sure, a creative activity often involves the transformation of natural objects, like the transformation of a slab of marble into Michelangelo's David. But even when confined to natural objects, creative activity is never naturalistic without remainder. The divine is always present at some level and indispensable." [8]

Fundraisers owe it to themselves to think about their attitude toward money and wealth. Attitude affects the spirit and purpose of our appeal to potential donors. Do we think in terms of mere accumulation of money, or do we see it as a gift from God? Remember it is the *love of money* that God abhors, not its possession. The people whom God blessed in Bible times were common people with uncommon love and respect for His authority over their economy and their day-to-day activities. They trusted Him to supply their resources and in return, expressed their thanksgiving in their worship and service.

> *"The measure of a life, after all, is not its duration, but it's donation."*
> —Corrie Ten Boom.

2. WE ARE IN A GROWTH PROCESS

Matthew 25:15, "To one he gave five bags of gold, to another two bags, and to another one bag, each according to his ability." The servants were learning how to carry out the master's orders. God's people were on a journey of physical and spiritual growth during their 400-year march to the Promised Land. I believe that faith is both an *event* and a *process*—the event of committing oneself to Christ is followed by a process of following and serving Him in all areas of life. The use of God's wealth is part of that process. "Each according to his ability" reflects a growth process of maturity. Nobel Prize winner Hermann Hesse wrote, "Maturity begins when one lives for others."

Obviously, my own journey to maturity hasn't been 400-years long (though my back feels like it after a day of carrying roofing shingles), but I'm familiar with *events* and *processes*. Let me illustrate. Marriage is both an event and a process. Our wedding day was an event I will never forget. It included a sacred ceremony with vows of love and willingness to serve each other. But it wasn't long into our marriage that I learned about the *process* of marriage, about putting our vows into practice—of trusting and serving and loving in daily living. And that is reminiscent of an earlier *event* in my life when I received my first allowance. My parents ceremoniously trusted me with money. But it was only the beginning of a management *process*. My home was a classroom where my teachers/parents taught me how to earn, save, and spend what God had entrusted to me. Every transaction from that time forward was influenced by what I learned then and there.

Verses 16-18, "The man who had received five bags of gold went at once and put his money to work and gained five bags more. So also, the one with two bags of gold gained two more. But the man who had received one bag went off, dug a hole in the ground and hid his master's money." It was a lesson in investment. The dictionary says investing is expending money with the expectation of achieving a profit or material result. It is never just about the moment and always about the future—added value. Fundraisers are futurists who lead their clientele to a stable, financial "promised land"—while working in a culture so unstable that it pays $690 billion in interest on credit card debt.

3. THE AMOUNT IS NOT IMPORTANT

Verses 19-21, "After a long time the master of those servants returned and settled accounts with them. The man who had received five bags of gold brought the other five. 'Master,' he said, 'you entrusted me with five bags of gold. See, I have gained five more.' His master replied, 'Well done, good and faithful servant! You have been faithful with a few things; I will put you in charge of many things. Come and share your master's happiness!'" The servants who brought an increase received the same affirmation

(v. 23), "Well done, good and faithful servant.'" The faithful in Bible times knew that God expected them to maximize and share their resources. Deuteronomy 15:11, "Since there will never cease to be some in need on the earth, I therefore command you, 'open your hand to the poor and needy neighbor in your land.'" The amount of the servant's return was not as important as his act of obedience. The beauty of God's principle of tithing is its non-discriminatory basis. The 10% standard is the same for the person listed in Fortune 500 as it is for the person in line for food stamps.

4. FAITH REQUIRES ACTION

Verse 24, "Then the man who had received one bag of gold came. 'Master,' he said, 'I knew that you are a hard man, harvesting where you have not sown and gathering where you have not scattered seed. So I was afraid and went out and hid your gold in the ground. See, here is what belongs to you.'"

People in Bible times knew that life isn't just in the knowing; it's in the knowing *and* doing. Once when Jesus was teaching, someone in the crowd yelled, "Blessed is the womb that bore You." Jesus answered, "Blessed rather are those who hear the word of God and obey it" (Luke 11:27-28). Researching financial principles and setting financial goals doesn't bring wealth without the *action* of good management. Nearly every person of wealth has a story of starting their financial journey with humble first steps. First. they envisioned, then they learned and grew, and finally they applied what they learned. Philanthropist John D. Rockefeller, Sr. said, "I never would have been able to tithe the first million dollars I have ever made if I had not tithed my first salary, which was $1.50 per week."

GREAT SPIRITUAL DEPRESSION

The culture of the ancients was agrarian. Land or animals were counted as wealth and used in payment or in the transfer. But tending the land

and animals in Bible times was grueling work—without the aid of John Deere diesel machinery or Silicon Valley technology that modern agriculture utilizes. Often their environment was perilous. Putting food on the table for their families was a selfless and loving task.

In one sense, the first family, Adam and Eve, set the tone for managing resources. They lived rent-free in the Garden of Eden and feasted on the food they never grew. That all changed when they committed the first sin (broke God's law on purpose) and decided to do life their way instead of God's. In financial terms, you might call it the "Great Spiritual Depression!" The bottom fell out of their "economy." Their growing "stock" in the Garden of Eden turned to penny stocks because they broke their "bonds" with God. The consequence was awful—spiritual separation from their Creator, loss of their home in the Garden, and a tiring new normal of a six-day workweek—for every week of their lives till death.

The cost of their sin was also "transferred" to the entire human race. What God said to them (Genesis 3:17, "Cursed is the ground because of you; through painful toil you will eat food from it all the days of your life.") became our reality. Every Monday morning of a tiring work week is forever linked to that first rebellion—as it certainly was for everyone living in Bible times. Generations to come would suffer from the effects of their decision. But God would not forget His covenant. Even then, God's love for them resulted in His supplying their needs. God is a Redeemer who is constantly leading His people toward their redemption. His faithfulness would grow other gardens. Build other homes. Increase other lands. Bless other families. And of course, provide redemption through the sacrificial death of His only Son, the Lord Jesus Christ.

That was the incomprehensible gift that anyone can receive without question. Let me try to illustrate it with a very personal story. One of my sons got into trouble at school, and it was serious enough that the principal notified his mother and me at home. We had a policy that if you got into trouble at school you would be in trouble at home. That night I told him to follow me to the bedroom to receive his punishment for breaking the school's rules. After reviewing the offense with him, I told him that he would be getting one whack with "The Paddle." The wooden, carved paddle was an "old school" memento I had kept from my time as a school principal in the 70s. (Today, it might either be a museum piece or evidence against corporal punishment by educational revisionists!) Frankly, it was rarely used in our home, but when the occasion presented itself, "The Paddle" would be pressed into service.

As I held the paddle in hand, my son looked at me and said, "Dad I don't want to take the whack with that paddle." My response was that the offense was serious enough to deserve punishment. I thought about it. I believed in discipline, but I also believed in mercy. Then, to his surprise, I said, "I'll take the punishment for you," handed the paddle to him and bent over the bed. What happened next is forever in my memory. He embraced me, and together we fell onto the bed weeping. There wasn't a paddling! I had never offered that proposition before and never offered it afterward. The mission was accomplished, the sacrifice was accepted.

About three months later I received a call from our youth pastor, David Kujawa, saying that my son had shared the story with the entire youth group, and added that he now had an idea of the love needed for Christ to take our punishment on the Cross. His story had a huge impact on the youth group and was later the subject of an article he wrote for a youth magazine. As parents, we do not always know the impact we are having on the next generation. Some things aren't seen at the time, but you can be sure that actions are the best way to say what's on our hearts.

GOD'S GOLD STANDARD

God always provides a plan of mercy and redemption. He put a system of wealth transfer in place that would provide resources to succeeding generations. His law of transfer was the gold standard. We see it on display when the daughters of one family contested an inheritance given to another family member. Numbers 27:5-11,

> So Moses brought their case before the Lord. And the Lord spoke to Moses, saying: "The daughters of Zelophehad speak what is right; you shall surely give them a possession of inheritance among their father's brothers, and cause the inheritance of their father to pass to them. And you shall speak to the children of Israel, saying: 'If a man dies and has no son, then you shall cause his inheritance to pass to his daughter. If he has no daughter, then you shall give his inheritance to his brothers. If he has no brothers, then you shall give his inheritance to his father's brothers. And if his father has no brothers, then you shall give his inheritance to the relative closest to him in his family, and he shall possess it.'" And it shall be to the children of Israel a statute of judgment, just as the Lord commanded Moses."

Additional laws of inheritance are listed in the Bible, including:

- The eldest son was to inherit a double portion, but Jewish tradition specified that only sons born before the death of the father were so privileged. (Deuteronomy 21:15-17).

- If there were no sons, daughters could inherit their father's land (Numbers 27:7-8).

- In the absence of direct heirs, a distant kinsman could inherit the land (Numbers 27:9-11).

- Because the land was given by God to individual families, the people were not allowed to dispose of their land permanently. If they needed to sell it, it was to be returned during the year of Jubilee (Leviticus 25:23-38).

The Levites had a very special and blessed inheritance from God: "The Levitical priests—including the whole tribe of Levi—are to have no allotment or inheritance with Israel. They shall live on the food offerings presented to the Lord, for that is their inheritance. (Deuteronomy 18:1-2).[9]

But the premise was the same: Every transfer must be in line with and in honor of the Creator. Jesus reminded us of that in the Lord's Prayer, which ends with the words, "For Yours is the kingdom and the power and the glory forever. Amen" (Matthew 6:13, NKJV).

BLESSING IN COMMANDS

Every command (or commandment) in the Bible springs from God's eternal love and is beneficial for those who obey. "The law of the LORD is perfect, refreshing the soul. The statutes of the LORD are trustworthy, making wise the simple" (Psalm 19:7). As an example, His laws of land management are highly practical and have been used throughout history in commerce and entrepreneurship. Blue said, "God's laws are timeless and transcendent, regardless of changing economic situations. Despite all the major economic and global changes, His principles still work." [10]

As with any law—including God's—breaking it is a possibility. Ancient times were not exempt. Since wealth was defined by the ownership of property used for agriculture, the wealthy often took advantage of the poor. They would give them loans, with the terms of the loans impossible for them to repay—and the land they owned was used as collateral. When the poor could not repay the loan, the lender would seize the land and the debtor would become a tenant or slave to the owner. This was one of the reasons the Bible condemns the exploitation of the poor.

"YEAR OF JUBILEE"

The way we manage our money can be just or unjust no matter the times. We cannot love God and exploit other people in our pursuit of wealth. Micah the prophet wrote, "What does the Lord require of you but to do justice, and to love kindness, and to walk humbly with your God?" (Micah 6:8). God's laws for His creation are behind every human cause aimed at protecting the planet. For example, In Old Testament times people were asked to observe a Sabbatical year, by leaving their land fallow. And every 50th Sabbatical year was called the "Year of Jubilee." During that time, all land was to be returned to its original owner—including an impoverished family member. In Leviticus 25:1-7 we see "bonus blessings" of the Year of Jubilee:

1. The jubilee tended to abolish poverty. It prevented large and permanent accumulations of wealth. It gave unfortunate families an opportunity to begin over again with a fair start in life. It particularly favored the poor, without injustice to the rich.

2. It tended to abolish slavery, and in fact, did abolish it; and it greatly mitigated it while it existed. "The effect of this law was at once to lift from the heart the terrible incubus of life-long bondage—that sense of a hopeless doom which knows no relief till death.

3. It was a provision of great wisdom for preserving families and tribes perfectly distinct, and their genealogies faithfully recorded, in order that all might have evidence to establish their right to the ancestral property.[11] Although we do not practice this strictly today, its principles form our teachings about wealth and its relation to our faith.

NEW TESTAMENT NUANCE

The New Testament landscape applied Old Testament practices in ways characteristic of its times. In New Testament writings, the Apostle Paul counsels the first-century church pastor, Timothy, to keep wealth in proper perspective (1 Timothy 6:6-19). To acknowledge that God gives an abundance to His people for their enjoyment. In 1 Timothy 6:17, he cautioned not to become overconfident in handling wealth, "Command those who are rich in this present world not to be arrogant nor to put their hope in wealth, which is so uncertain, but to put their hope in God, who richly provides us with everything for our enjoyment." James the apostle even addressed preferential seating arrangements. James 2:1-4,

"We are most like God when we give."
– Gordon MacDonald

My brothers and sisters, believers in our glorious Lord Jesus Christ must not show favoritism. Suppose a man comes into your meeting wearing a gold ring and fine clothes, and a poor man in filthy old clothes also comes in. If you show special attention to the man wearing fine clothes and say, "Here's a good seat for you," but say to the poor man, "You stand there" or "Sit on the floor by my feet," have you not discriminated among yourselves and become judges with evil thoughts?

JESUS THE MANAGER

The life of Jesus was a perfect model for managing resources. Leaving heaven's throne to live among people, He was raised in the home of a carpenter. A simple life for a Sovereign! Understanding the hardships of humanity, His teachings provided a NEW look at the Old Testament lifestyles of the faithful. He was the onsite fulfillment of the Kingdom, "the visible image of the invisible God. He existed before anything was created and is supreme over all creation" (Colossians 1:15).

- He acknowledged the supply of His heavenly Father. "Jesus then took the loaves, gave thanks, and distributed to those who were seated" (John 6:11).

- He had a minimalist lifestyle. "Jesus replied, 'Foxes have dens and birds have nests, but the Son of Man has no place to lay his head'" (Luke 9:58).

- He practiced and taught compassion for the poor. "The Spirit of the Lord is on me, because he has anointed me to proclaim good news to the poor" (Luke 4:18).

- He taught responsible citizenship. "Give back to Caesar what is Caesar's, and to God what is God's" (Matthew 22:21).

- He practiced and taught the laws of giving, including the tithe. "Woe to you, teachers of the law and Pharisees, you hypocrites! You give a tenth of your spices—mint, dill and cumin. But you have neglected the more important matters of the law—justice, mercy and faithfulness. You should have practiced the latter, without neglecting the former" (Matthew 23:23).

- He taught that material possessions threaten allegiance to God. "The worries of this life, the deceitfulness of wealth and the desires for other things come in and choke the word, making it unfruitful" (Mark 4:19).

- He urged His followers to minister to the needy. "Give to the one who asks you, and do not turn away from the one who wants to borrow from you" (Matthew 5:42).

- He obeyed Old Testament law with great respect. "Do not think that I have come to abolish the Law or the Prophets; I have not come to abolish them but to fulfill them" (Matthew 5:17).

When we think of Who He was (and is) and what He did (and does), we can relate when John the disciple and gospel writer seemed to throw in the literary towel in trying to sum up Christ's life. John 21:25, "Jesus did many other things as well. If every one of them were written down, I suppose that even the whole world would not have room for the books that would be written."

COMMUNITY OF BELIEVERS

His disciples followed His lead. Dropping their fishing nets in the sands of time, they followed Jesus and His message to their very death—all but one dying a martyr, and that one dying exiled on an island. They were very human, with human passions and ambitions, but they taught us how to "Seek first the kingdom of God and His righteousness" (Matthew 6:33). Following the crucifixion and resurrection of Jesus, His followers/disciples became a growing community of believers. Meeting in humble house churches, they studied and prayed and ministered to others in the power of the Holy Spirit. They received their instruction from the parchment scrolls of Scripture writers and shared letters from such leaders as the Apostles Paul, John, Luke, James, and Peter.

They pooled their resources—often selling their homes to provide food and shelter for other Christ-followers and house churches, ministered to the poor from the sale of their properties and other sacrificial gifts, and practiced tithing. We can't imagine the majority of them being "wealthy," but surely, they transferred what resources they had to their children according to God's Inheritance laws. And surely they were in line for God's Great Handoff, "Whoever has forsaken houses, or brothers or sisters, or father or mother, or children or lands, for my sake, shall receive many times as much and shall have as his inheritance the Life of the Ages" (Matthew 19:29). They lived sacrificially and ministered extravagantly. Those who had more learned how to live with less. And those who actually were wealthy learned about eternal riches in following Jesus. People followed Him because they saw His characteristics in the lives of His disciples. Leaders like John the Baptist taught the importance of caring for the needy, "Anyone who has two shirts should share with the one who has none, and anyone who has food should do the same" (Luke 3:11).

How would that play out today? I was interested to learn more about what's called the "Sharing Economy." Caitlin Burke called it "one of the fastest-growing business trends in history," where people are renting or borrowing goods rather than buying or owning them. They are sharing things like cars, spare rooms, offices, and even church space. The dictionary defines it as an economic activity that involves individuals buying or selling access to goods or services especially as arranged through an online company or organization. Burke says she was praying about opening a co-working space for her women clients when she heard about it. That led her to a company called Church Space. Its mobile app "connects vacant church spaces with ministries, business owners, and event professionals seeking space at an affordable rate." Church groups who could not afford to equip a facility can reserve and rent one that is fully equipped. Unused space in church (empty classrooms, basements, unused areas) can be turned into community event centers for Bible study, art studios or exercise classes—all doing ministry in space that would be otherwise empty.[12] The community of believers in the first-century church had a "sharing economy." And once again, we see proof that the Kingdom of Heaven is an eternally relevant and forward kingdom that is a proven source for financial wisdom or anything else.

PASSING THE TEST

God continues to bless His people in obedience to their faith and their giving. His law of the tithe challenges us. He said, "test Me in this. . . and see if I will not throw open the floodgates of heaven and pour out so much blessing that there will not be room enough to store it." I often use this passage when speaking on fundraising. Sometimes the blessings are "in-kind," a modern fundraising term. I've used it to ask donors to give our organization an item needed for its operation. Items like asking a florist to give flowers for decorating a building or office and asking a car dealership to loan a vehicle to an organization for the use of its staff. Because ancient peoples were subsistence farmers, the people of the Bible also experienced God's gifts-in-kind—such as the blessings of rains or sunshine to increase their crop yield. God will always fulfill His part of the "Test Me" challenge—and we will run out of room to store it. In my book, *It's Not About the Money*, I illustrated how if all Christians in America gave according to their ability and to God's command in the Scriptures, annual giving by Christians would be approximately $85.5 billion.

- $10 billion would provide care for 20 million children for a year.

- $330 million would back 150,000 missionaries in countries closed to religious workers.

- $2.2 billion would triple the funding of Bible translation, printing, and distribution.

- $600 million would start eight Christian colleges in Eastern Europe and Southeast Asia.

We would change the world with $85.5 billion—if we just followed God's command to give. There's a legendary story (neither factual nor biblical) about a wealthy man who couldn't wait to see what his home in heaven would look like. When he suddenly arrived there, he was taken on a tour. The first mansion was spectacular. "Is that mine?" he asked the angel guide. "No," the guide replied, "The owner was a gardener." The new arrival thought, "Wow! If a gardener's mansion looks like that, what must my mansion look like!"

The tour of spectacular mansions continued—the orphanage teacher, the farmer, and the factory worker's mansions. Finally, they came to a mansion under construction. "Who will live there?" the angel guide was asked, and then replied, "Oh, that will be yours, Sir." The astonished man said, "Mine? It's not even finished!" And the angels said, "I'm sorry, but with what you've sent us to work with, that's as far as we got."

Gordon MacDonald wrote, "Following God's example, the generous giver gives out of his or her very best. God gave His only Son; we give from the depths of our resources and abilities. . . As God sacrificed His Son, so we follow and give even those things that are most precious to us in our personal worlds. . . As biblical people, we believe that a solid proportion of our giving should move in the direction of those activities that make Christ known." [13] There is a very stirring scene in the Old Testament book of Deuteronomy. The Creator and Owner of all the earth starts the conversation with a reminder, includes instructions for sacrificial giving, and then ends with a call to worship,

> He brought us to this place and gave us this land flowing with milk and honey! And now, O Lord, I [Moses] have brought you the first portion of the harvest you have given me from the ground.' Then place the produce before the Lord your God, and bow to the ground in worship before him (Deuteronomy 26:9-10, NLT).

May it be so in our lives as well.

Fundraising in a Christian context is exciting. It combines the best of what God offers with the best that people decide to offer. And it not only benefits those of us who match gifts with organizations that need it, but it also enriches others in a great cycle of giving. As Vice president for Advancement at Indiana Wesleyan University, it was often my privilege to take alumni on tours of the new or remodeled buildings on the 320-acre main campus. One tour stop was the John Wesley building. The oldest building on campus (1896), it received a $3 million-plus renovation and continues to be a special place—including a bust of the noted 18th Century theologian, evangelist, and reformer, John Wesley in the foyer. Nearly every student who attended IWU has been in that building, but it was always a joy to see the faces of alumni as they saw the renovations. A beautiful new board room occupies the area on the 3rd floor that once housed the chapel. So, for students who went to chapel there, that is the area most wanted to see.

Memories from the past are almost visible on their countenance. I remember taking Ron and Marge there. Tears welled in Ron's eyes as the 90-year-old alum walked to a spot in the room and said, "This is where I made my decision to follow Christ." We wept together, both of us knowing it was probably one of the last times he would be on the campus. I had visited Ron and Marge in their Florida assisted living apartment several times and helped them establish a missionary scholarship fund for IWU. I was blessed to see how much it meant to both of them to be on campus—and see their investment at work.

A little while later, another alum toured the building. Dr. Melvin Gentry, a retired minister and former pastor of the college church, walked to a back corner of the room and pointed, "Right about here… this is where I knelt when I received my call to the ministry." So many lives… so many stories, it reminded me of the Geron Davis lyrics to the familiar song, "We are standing on holy ground, and I know that there are angels all around; let us praise Jesus now, we are standing in His presence on holy ground." [14] I don't know if buildings have a legacy like people have legacies, but I know that those days touring the 3rd floor of the John Wesley building were very special times—in a very special place.

That must have been the feeling of people in Old Testament time who gave of their time and resources in building the Temple in Jerusalem. As they visited it, areas of the building would hold special memories of their sacrifice and its blessing. And that must be the feeling of fundraisers when they visit places made possible by the gifts of people—places so vital in the lives of those who benefited from them.

"What counts in life is not the mere fact that we have lived.
It is what difference we have made to the lives of others."
– Nelson Mandela

CHAPTER 3

Building a Personal Legacy

Lee J. Colan wrote about a man nicknamed "Easy Eddie." Eddie was Al Capone's personal lawyer and was skilled in keeping the infamous gangster out of jail. Capone rewarded him with wealth, funding "Easy Eddie's" mansion in Chicago. But the rough-living lawyer had one soft spot—a dearly loved son. Eddie did his best to teach his son right from wrong but began to realize that even with all his wealth, he couldn't pass along a good name to him. So "Easy Eddie" decided to go straight—to try to clear his name by telling the authorities about Capone. He did it, knowing it would cost him his life—which it did in a blaze of gunfire. He paid the ultimate price to give his son the legacy of a good name.

During World War II, a pilot and Lieutenant Commander in the US Navy named Butch O'Hare became a war hero. Flying with his squadron, his plane was nearly empty of fuel and he was ordered to leave the squadron and return to the aircraft carrier when suddenly a large formation of Japanese aircraft appeared. O'Hare knew they were heading for the Navy fleet, but he couldn't warn them or his squadron because of a damaged radio. Butch fired on the enemy until his ammunition was gone—and then bravely decided to fly directly into their formation, successfully diverting them. Making it back to the carrier, film in the camera attached to a wing of his plane revealed that he had destroyed five enemy aircraft.

Lieutenant Commander Butch O'Hare was designated the first "Ace" in the war and given a Congressional Medal of Honor. He was later killed in battle, and his hometown honored his bravery by naming an airport after him—Chicago O'Hare International Airport. "Easy Eddie" had given his son a legacy that has affected generations since. The lesson: "Inheritance is what we leave to others. Legacy is what we leave IN them." [15]

Fundraisers have an opportunity to practice what they *reach*. That may be a lame turnaround on the familiar "practice what you preach," but I think it reminds us to make sure we are practicing wise money management. Otherwise, a "leg" will be missing in our "legacy." We are major players in the Great Handoff. In my profession, over the years I have raised funds for numerous buildings without any hands-on participation in their construction. But personally, I've been involved in countless construction projects. From that perspective, I've observed that building a personal legacy and building a house have a lot in common. I see seven steps to building a personal legacy: Drawing the plans; Determining the cost; Ordering materials; Laying the foundation; Framing the structure; Enclosing the structure; and the Final inspection.

1. DRAWING THE PLANS.

Modern CAD (computer-aided design) drawings have simplified the process of drawing plans, but the programs would be useless without examples, vision, and a direction. The CAD software builder, program, and programmer are part of the process. In my life, the initial step is trust in the

Creator of the minds who create the programs. God promised, "I will guide you along the best pathway for your life. I will advise you and watch over you" (Psalm 32:8, NLT). My mom and dad practiced that—and handed it off to me. Although raised in a very modest home with no frills, and with parents who worked tirelessly to provide for my four siblings and me, I am grateful that they modeled frugality in their living and generosity in their giving. Whether it was sharing vegetables from the garden, sitting with a sick friend, or dropping extra dollars in the offering plate, my parents gave as selflessly as possible without any thought of return.

> *"One of the best ways to teach a child anything is by doing it yourself. Your child will see what you do and copy it."*
> – David Leads

Studies show that parents who give make a major impact on whether their children will also be givers. Money management, then, is a Great Handoff. It has been said that 55% of people with over $1 million in inheritance talk to their children about their finances and their estate, while 53% with less than $1 million don't. Reasons given include:

1. They don't want to confront dying.

2. They are uncomfortable disclosing financial matters.

3. They don't want their children to know what they are going to receive.

4. They are concerned with their heirs' ability to handle the inheritance.

We generally think of an inheritance as the transfer of financial assets; however, an even greater transfer is passing along values and life lessons.

The Munday family has traditions that are extremely important. Some are fun and funny, while others are spiritual and nostalgic. I hope our children will always remember them. I'm glad to be a part of those traditions, but I would prefer to be remembered as a generous father and grandfather who not only gave to my family but also to Christian causes and others in need. Blair Schiff wrote about the need for teaching the next generations about wise financial management in *Fox Business Insider*. He quoted Charles Schwab, "Schools don't teach financial literacy, so, it's I think, a national problem that kids are not doing what they should early in their lives… they don't really find out about investing or what the responsibility is for them to do until they're maybe 30 years of age." [16]

When they review my IRS forms and financial statements, I want my heirs to know that my relationship with Christ impacted how I invested or spent God's money. If it causes them to follow my example, that is my legacy. I've heard it said that you can see a person's heart through their checkbook. It is important that we model giving for the next generation— "Teaching by doing." I want giving to become a habit with my children and grandchildren.

Draw your legacy. Plan the future of your financial house before you advise others on the details of theirs. We are creating a legacy on a daily basis—and leaving it to our families, our community, and our world. A legacy has many shapes and sizes.

- Strong leadership.
- Large bank accounts.
- Endurance over suffering.
- Love for others.

Some are very positive and others negative. Our society has conditioned us to think of legacy as wealth and money but there is more. It also includes our experiences, the wisdom we learned, and times shared with friends and family that creates memories and transforms lives. Someone wisely said, "A good example has twice the value of good advice." Good plans result in good buildings—dependable, secure, friendly, accessible, attractive buildings. A good legacy has those same qualities. Leave a good legacy as a fundraiser. Who you are will be even more important than what you have done.

- Character is capital.

- Wisdom is wealth.

- Kindness is an investment.

- Acceptance is equity.

2. DETERMINE THE COST

With a 4 x 8 sheet of plywood that can cost as much as $30 and a 2 x 4 x 8 piece of lumber that can run up to $4, cost is a huge factor in the building process. Building a legacy is even more crucial—and costlier. There was an interesting scene in the "Saving Private Ryan" movie about a soldier who had 3 siblings in the war. The Army wanted to prevent his death so his mother wouldn't have to experience the possibility of losing all her sons. An Army captain and a platoon were sent to find him and bring him home. Once they found him, Private Ryan refused to go home, saying it was his duty to fight. In the final scene of the movie, the mortally wounded Captain John Miller reflecting on the death of soldiers on his team, says with his last breaths, "Earn this." In other words, spend the rest of your life repaying those who died by living a life worth saving. As Christians we could never earn our salvation; we are saved by grace, but as Christians, we are also expected to serve and sacrifice—to live our lives as proof we were worth saving. Philippians 3:16, "Let us live up to what we have already attained."

I like the story of the business owner who came home from a long day at the office to find a normally neat house looking like a hurricane had swept through it. The children were still in their pajamas stacking food boxes in the living room. A lamp was laying on the floor where it had been knocked over. A throw rug was wadded up against the wall. And an unwatched TV was blaring. When his wife entered the room, her husband said, "What in the world happened here? Are you okay?" She calmly explained, "Yes. It's just that nearly every day you walk through the door you ask me what I did all day. Well, today I didn't do it!"

"Earning it" is doing what we do with the skills we have. And it is part of the legacy we pass along to our heirs. Fundraising is a difficult job that requires a 24/7 commitment to bring about excellent results. Being a good fundraiser requires that person to be very proactive. To demonstrate I emphasize that there are two ways to get to the top of an oak tree. You can climb the tree, or you can sit on an acorn. The latter is not satisfactory for fundraisers. They must be proactive, they must climb the tree. The closer one gets to the retirement years the personal cost is not commensurate with those of the earlier years. And retirement opens (and closes) financial options. Of all people, fundraisers should understand the importance of planning for retirement. And they should also know that planning includes developing a giving strategy. During the working years, giving is driven by the need. Retirement allows more time to think strategically about giving. What organizations will I be able to help support? What values am I transferring in my giving? What is the best way to involve my family members in my giving?

"You have not lived until you have done something for someone who can never repay you."
– John Bunyan

I knew a couple who built a nice nest egg for retirement. They had exercised restraint and frugality as an approach to life. Both had served as professional teachers and used all their extra money to purchase farmland. They bought only the necessities of life and always received 2-3 quotes for any work on their property—even on items that cost only $500 to repair. Each time I asked them for a gift, they would respond by saying, "as soon as our ship comes in, your charity will be the first to know."

The father died of cancer, and about two years later the mother passed. The couple had two sons who had good jobs, but each had experienced a failure in their marriages. A short time after the death of the parents, I received a visit from one son, who was now driving a black BMW with all the luxury options you could imagine. I inquired about his job. He had a professional job that paid higher than the average wage. So, I was surprised when his reply was "I quit. I am the executor of mom and dad's estate and I wanted to make certain everything was completed correctly." He added, "Unlike Mom and Dad, I want to have some fun during my lifetime. You know they worked so hard and never had the opportunity to enjoy life?" I learned later that he had spent most of his parents' estate and had not been able to find a job that met his "level of interest."

The scenario is not uncommon, especially when parents fail to understand the dangers of passing wealth to their children. I have been told there is a 70% failure rate when transferring family wealth from one generation to another. In most cases, it is a result of poor investments or poor management. Parents fail to share financial information with their children that would prepare them for the handoff. This is not only a major financial blunder but could lead to a disaster. Parents seem to put these "tough talks" off until a later time, a time that never occurs. Face it, we are afraid to discuss money matters with the family.

My experience is that there is at least one child in each family who has money management problems or a personality that does not promote compromise. Who gets dad's tools, mom's rings and jewelry, the heirlooms hanging on the wall in the living room? It is not always about the money; it is about the sentimental value. My wife has spent many hours cutting and pasting Creative Memory pictures in books during our 51 years of marriage and my daughters have already laid claim to those family memories—and yes, they have been allocated in our will.

Fundraisers must understand that people may work hard all their life and meet all their financial obligations but fail to leave a legacy that will outlive them or outlive the next generation. For that reason, I advise those making estate plans to consider leaving at least a tithe of their estate to a charity. Most of these individuals have tithed their entire lives. But they have a great opportunity to send a message to their heirs of what was most important during their life—and that is legacy building. Better yet, in the case just sighted, the estate could have been divided, giving each son a third and giving a third to charity. It would have been a great way to emphasize the importance of giving to something that will outlive them. Both parents had lived godly lives and would be disappointed to know their money was being spent in this fashion. In fact, there is a good chance that they unwittingly contributed to their son's spiritual demise!

In almost every presentation I give, I open with two quotes. The first is from Andrew Carnegie who realized the impact that wealth can have on children, "The almighty dollar bequeathed to a child is an almighty curse. No man has the right to handicap his son with such a burden as great wealth. Will my fortune be safe with my son and will my son be safe with my fortune?" The second is from William K. Vanderbilt (grandson of Cornelius Vanderbilt), "Inherited wealth is as certain death to ambition as cocaine is to morality." I have read (and experienced) many stories where the wealthy have passed huge holdings to their heirs, only to find that by the second or third generation, the wealth had been squandered—and often the family had to file for bankruptcy.

Someone once said that an airplane will burn the greatest amount of its fuel during takeoff, and less when it reaches its cruising altitude. The same is true with wealth; it takes a lot more effort to build than it does to maintain. People who suddenly inherit wealth stand a greater risk of losing it because they fail to understand the basics of spending less than they earn. As an example, it is estimated that over 25% of lottery winners go bankrupt.

There is always a cost to greatness. Ask the athletes alone in the gym lifting weights or practicing foul shots or practicing on the balance beam long after the rest of the team has gone home. They aren't there because it is something to do, they are there because there is something to BE—on the center step of the medal ceremony platform. Legacy costs. The poet Maya Angelou said, "You shouldn't go through life with a catcher's mitt on both hands. You need to be able to throw something back." Jesus called His disciples to a life of obscurity and hardship. Had they not accepted the challenge, they might have lived and died without anyone except their own family knowing their name. Their renown was the result of their resolve to pay the cost that leaves the legacy, responding to the call to move beyond what they used to be or what they were to what they could become.

I read about Steve Jobs' desire to have a strong marketing program and the best marketer for his Macintosh computer release. He approached John Sculley, President of Pepsi-Cola. Scully had a great salary, a beautiful Connecticut home, and no desire to leave his position. When Jobs persisted with the hiring attempt, Scully said he would need a salary of $1 million, a $1 million signing bonus and $1 million in severance if the job fell through. They negotiated back and forth and were at an impasse. In one last attempt to hire Scully, Jobs asked for a face-to-face meeting and asked the question that became one of the most quotable quotes in business journalism, "Do you want to spend the rest of your life selling sugared water or do you want a chance to change the world." The question startled John Scully and he took the job, and under his management, turned Apple's $800 million in sales into $8 billion The question could be asked in a different circumstance for everyone who wants to build a personal legacy. "Do you want to stay where you are, doing what you do, or do you want to change the world?"

3. ORDER MATERIALS

The wise estimation and purchase of materials in construction projects can bring the project happily *within* or wildly *over* budget. The unwise estimate and purchase can send the costs higher than the roof of the building under construction. Fundraisers are not just advisors; they are examples in their own management of funds. The warning in the old proverb, "it is better to avoid a dangerous situation than to confront it" is amplified in spending carelessly. Warren Buffet, who is currently the third richest man in America lives in his original Nebraska home, which was purchased for $31,500 in 1958. And it's said that he has used the same wallet for 20 years, eats at McDonald's for breakfast, and still uses a flip phone. More than likely, Buffet spends his money on assets that appreciate rather than depreciate. Did his conservative approach to living bring him his great wealth? Not by itself, but his modest spending has increased it. Thomas Stanley and William Danko noted in their book, *The Millionaire Next Door*, that most millionaires live in average neighborhoods, drive average cars, and work average jobs. However, they keep their spending in check. The authors described the affluent as "frugal, frugal, frugal."

I'm certainly not in the Buffet neighborhood of financial rankings, but what I have gained has certainly not been because I made budget-*busting* choices. Most think I made my money by working as a vice-president at Indiana Wesleyan University. Actually, I made it by buying rental houses on a mortgage, fixing them up and making most of the repairs by myself evenings after a workday and on Saturdays. On any weeknight, you could find me either in a crawl space under the house, on the floor under a sink inside the house, or climbing a ladder to the roof of the house—often stringing lights so I could stretch a day into a late evening. And when my children went along, those projects turned into teaching times.

I remember one incident with fondness. My son Michael asked to help me run heat ducts under a house. I started the project and then looked for something he could do that would be a teaching moment. At about eight o'clock, I called for him to hold up one end of a pipe while I held the other. There was a long pause, and then a search for the missing member of my "work team." I soon found him—using his arm for a pillow while he took an after-dinner siesta. Of course, my Parent-self took over the Jobsite-self. The heat duct could wait, but the sleepy son was past his school night bedtime. Whether "sleeping on the job" or not, Michael said he learned skills from me that he later used working on his own house. I was always concerned with passing what I had or what I learned along to my family. So, I've always been cautious about "ordering materials" in my long-term retirement plan and leaving an inheritance to my family. In the process, I've found that choosing to put the discretion in "discretionary spending" pays a bonus.

After the purchase and renovation of one house, I would have it appraised to enable the purchase of another, and on and on, until I had acquired 40 rental homes. To expedite the progress, I amortized all the houses with a five-year payoff. I didn't have time for many extracurricular activities—only the basics, and often I would feel guilty for being away from my wife and children. But for the most part, I'm sure they knew it wasn't about me just gathering resources; it was about them—generating extra income for everyday living costs.

> *"Few actions of consequence in the world have been accomplished without passion"*
> – Jerold Panas

4. LAYING THE FOUNDATION.

Most of us who have spent time in Sunday school remember Sunday school songs. One stands out in my mind, "The wise man built his house upon a rock?" The next verse said, "The foolish man built his house upon the sand." You might remember what happened after "the rains came down and the floods came up." The wise man's house stood firm, while the foolish man's house fell flat. No matter the height or beauty of a structure, a faulty foundation will result in its eventual ruin. That goes for legacy-building as well. The millions of dollars in gifts to institutions that I have facilitated have come from my lifetime commitment to serving the Lord with the resources He has loaned to me. I am a steward/manager of those resources, responsible to build my financial house on the rock.

The unexpected blessing of those ventures? They made me a better fundraiser and, more importantly, made me a more charitable person. As a former track coach, I like the story of Roger Bannister, the British middle-distance runner who ran the first 4-minute mile at the 1952 Olympics in Helsinki. We remember the name and the record 3:59.4 seconds (a record that was broken 46 days later), but we may have forgotten a couple of related facts. One, he didn't win Olympic Gold; he finished fourth in the British record-breaking 1500 meters. Two, his lasting fame was not in "the run," it was in saving lives and training physicians as a distinguished neurologist at Oxford's Pembroke College, until his retirement in 1993. When asked about his achievement, he said he would rather be known for his contribution to academic medicine.[17]

Like Bannister, I want my life to be known for more than one run, for instance, meeting a fundraising goal. I want to aid the cause of Christian education for a lifetime to the glory of Christ. On one occasion I was asked to assist a Christian school in buying a building. A donor had provided $750,000 as a lead gift, but the purchase of the building required $1 million. That meant that an additional $250,000 needed to be raised as a challenge. The donor wanted the Christian school to have a building without debt. He asked me to, first, challenge the board and, second, to help identify individuals within the school community that could help it reach the $250,000 challenge match. The donor had offered to pay my fee to help the school. So, the following Thursday night I met with the school board and told them that I had an anonymous donor who would give $750,000, but the board would be required to raise the additional $250,000. Combined, that would completely pay for the building—and no debt would be incurred. What a blessing it was as the fundraiser to go to a Christian school needing $1 million dollars and offer $750,000 toward the project. It was a fundraiser's dream come true! And as frosting on the cake, I was able to tell the board that the donor was going to pay my counseling fee to raise the money.

I then told the board members I would return at the next board meeting, scheduled a week later, to find out what commitment the board was willing to make, and for the names of individuals whom I could approach to help raise the remaining funds. The following Thursday I received word that members of the eight-member board would give a total of $50,000. That night the board also identified additional people from the school community that might be prospective donors for us to call. Returning to the donor to share the good news, I asked him if he had individuals within his purview that might also be prospects. With some hesitation, he provided two names and I asked if he or the principal of the school would join me to share the vision of the school and I would make the Ask.

The donor agreed to accompany me on the first visit and did a great job of telling the prospective donor why he felt the school would be a good investment for the community and the advancement of Christian education. The prospective donor said he was interested in the project because his grandchildren attended the school. I followed with the Ask for $250,000. The prospective donor responded that he would consult with his wife and would let us know within a week. We thanked him for his interest, and I left my business card. The following Wednesday I received a check in the mail for $150,000. What a praise! Our first Ask and we had already received more than half of the total money needed!

The second visit with the donor was scheduled, and I was accompanied by the school principal. The principal shared the vision and I made the Ask for $250,000. The owners of the business and their two daughters were in the room. They were enthusiastic at the prospect of their grandchildren having a nice facility in which to receive a Christian education but said they needed a week to make the decision. We decided to meet in the same room at 10:00 a.m. one week later. And in that meeting, they revealed that they would make an additional donation of $100,000. You may wonder why in two Asks I would seek the total amount needed? We realized that additional funds would be needed to get the school ready for occupancy. But we had accomplished our goal and had raised the money necessary to meet the initial challenge.

Now, the surprise "reveal." The donor who had asked me to help with the campaign asked for my fees and I told him there would be none. I explained that his gift had made the difference in many young children's lives and that would be payment enough for me. That December, approximately 3-4 months later, I received a letter in the mail from him, stating that their company had experienced a good year and that he and his wife wanted to bless my wife and me with a Christmas gift of $25,000. Although not expecting the gift, what my friends didn't know was that I had made two pledges for the year: one to my church for $15,000 and a second to a Bible college for $10,000. Knowing that both pledges would need to be paid by December 31, I had contemplated which of my houses I would sell to fulfill my commitment. That donor instantly put the "fun" in "fundraising!" And once again, I had lost a giving competition with my heavenly Father! Isn't God good! The Scripture that says He will supply all our needs according to His riches had come true—again. Luke 6:38 had been fulfilled before my very eyes, "For if you give, you will get! Your gift will return to you in full and overflowing measure, pressed down, shaken together to make room for more, and running over." This has been a blessing that I have experienced over and over during my 30 years of serving God as a fundraiser.

Early in my career at Indiana Wesleyan University, I needed reliable transportation to travel the many miles to meet with prospective donors. I called a local car dealer, DeVoe Chevrolet-Cadillac, and asked if they had a car I could use to represent the school in my fundraising efforts. Approximately two weeks later, I received a telephone call asking me to come to the dealership—and that a brand-new white Cadillac would be ready for my use. They had gone far beyond my expectations, but I had to tell them that even though I was overwhelmed by their generous offer, donors might be turned off if I were to visit them driving such an expensive car. A short time later they asked me to come back and inquired if I could drive a Chevrolet Astro van. I immediately responded that it would be perfect—and for the next 15 years, they supplied me with a new van each year, fully loaded, at no cost to the university. What a tremendous blessing.

Investment wise, putting your faith in the Lord Jesus Christ will result in returns beyond counting. Never once have I ever heard someone say they were sorry they made the decision to use their life and skills in His service. But too many times I have heard someone's regret that they hadn't— or that they had waited so long. Frankly, there have been more bonuses than barriers. For example, after helping a nonprofit in Indianapolis with their fundraising, its president asked me to play golf. I said that I wasn't very good, but I enjoyed playing. She then said she had a golf partner from Texas in mind for the match but wanted me to guess who it might be—and added, "Think big!" I thought about it and finally named Jerry Jones, the Dallas Cowboys owner. She responded, "Think bigger." I told her the only Texan I could think of that was any bigger than Jones was President George Bush. "Correct!" she said and told me the arrangement was being made.

Unfortunately, the President was unable to join us for that round because his father, President George H. W. Bush had been admitted to the hospital. But later I received a call saying the President would be coming to Indianapolis to play at the Crooked Stick Golf course and I was invited to play. As a former history teacher, I couldn't let my golf game insecurities interfere with such a historic meeting. The President was very kind, and we traded signed books. Later he sent me a letter thanking me for the book. Fundraising can be a difficult job, but it will give you opportunities you never dreamed you would have.

GEORGE W. BUSH

September 23, 2011

Mr. Terry T. Munday
Marion, Indiana

Dear Terry:

Thank you for the warm welcome to Indianapolis. I enjoyed my trip. I only wish I had a little more time to visit.

Thanks, too, for the copy of *It's Not About The Money*. It looks like an interesting read.

Laura and I send our best wishes.

Sincerely,

George W. Bush

5. FRAMING THE STRUCTURE

The layout of any building isn't accidental. Much thought is given to the best use of its square footage, how much space will be given to each room, what will go where, and how will that space compliment or serve the total building. Building the structure is totally essential to the remainder of the building. What does a floor plan and structure have to do with building a legacy? The Scriptures say that by faith in the Lord Jesus Christ, we are "being built together to become a dwelling in which God lives by his Spirit" (Ephesians 2:22). If you are building a legacy you will need to allocate "living space" for spiritual growth, learning, fellowship, family time, and recreation. Jesus lived a perfectly planned life. The Bible says He grew in "wisdom, and stature, and in favor with God and man" (Luke 2:52).

Omit space for any of those areas, and you will be less-equipped to build a legacy for your heirs—or build a reputation among your peers or clientele. The demands of fundraising can be . . . well, demanding! Success in business isn't based on busyness alone. It incorporates a legacy-building lifestyle that focuses on your most important associates—your family and friends.

> *There are two ways of spreading light: to be the candle or the mirror that reflects it.*
> – Edith Wharton

At the age of 72, I have spent quite a bit of time reflecting on God's goodness to me and the blessing of family. Some family memories are like the framework in a house—each providing a supporting permanence:

- Grandpa Dugan sitting on the porch at Faith Cottage singing gospel songs and choruses.

- My children playing in sports competitions.

- Traveling across the country in a crowded (12 people), homemade camper.

- Family sing-a-longs in the back of a truck—especially the Christmas caroling.

- My children and grandchildren singing songs of the church while leading worship.

- My grandchildren marching across the stage to receive academic awards.

None of those activities required a large expenditure of money, but I consider them priceless. Since my wife and I are privileged to live within three miles of our children and grandchildren, we have almost daily interaction with them. Passing along a legacy with eternal values is far more important than a temporal inheritance of money. I challenge you to build your framework with "treated wood," material of eternal value that lasts in spite of the storms. Add framing for the windows for God's light to shine through. Install doorways that will open to those who need to hear the gospel and see it at work in your life.

6. ENCLOSING THE STRUCTURE.

After the electric, plumbing, and heating have been installed, the walls are next to take shape. Sheetrock over the required insulation and then siding, combine to keep the warmth in and the cold out. They also protect the residents from the undesirable element that would like to make their way into the house. In one sense, your house is your fortress. Its walls are like castle walls "in days of yore," keeping the enemy from overtaking its residents. And like those same days, you will not only need tall and sturdy walls, you will need to be fitted with a suit of armor to protect them. But to my knowledge, the only armor worthy to withstand enemy attack isn't available at the mall and can't be ordered online. The Bible says to, "Put on the full armor of God, so that you can take your stand against the devil's schemes. For our struggle is not against flesh and blood, but against the rulers, against the authorities, against the powers of this dark world and against the spiritual forces of evil in the heavenly realms" (Ephesians 6:11-12). Spiritual darkness has a singular mission: to extinguish the light of God's Word. Spiritual armor is the only proven protection—and the Sword of God's Spirit (the Bible) is the only proven weapon.

It reminds me of a story about a donor named Lee who came to my office and wanted to build a new art building on campus, a great need since the old building that housed the art department was over 100 years old. He had three major requirements: 1. The new building would be built with frugality, 2. that it would be built economically, and 3. that it would be built WITHOUT WINDOWS. We tried to build all facilities on campus with those first two principles in mind, but building an art building without windows would not be possible. After a few meetings and some compromise, he agreed to build the art building with both windows and brick rather than a metal structure—and gave the university over $3 million dollars. A building with walls but no windows or light would be impractical. Similarly, a legacy without spiritual walls or windows or light would not just be impractical, it would be vulnerable.

I've always admired the prophet, Nehemiah. He had such a passion for rebuilding the protective walls of Jerusalem that had been destroyed by enemy armies and left unrepaired, that he abandoned the comforts of life in the court of a king to devote himself to rebuilding them. Nehemiah 4:6 is a progress report, "We rebuilt the wall till all of it reached half its height, for the people worked with all their heart." And verses 21-22 tell us the reason the job was completed, "we continued the work with half the men holding spears, from the first light of dawn till the stars came out. At that time I also said to the people, 'Have every man and his helper stay inside Jerusalem at night, so they can serve us as guards by night and as workers by day.'" The spiritual application is awesome.

- Vision: walls that needed restoration.

- Planning: guards by night and workers by day.

- Determination: from the light of dawn till the stars came out.

Every fundraiser needs a vision, a plan, and a determination to build the walls of a spiritual character in an age of moral apathy. Finish well by starting right. And whatever you'll need, God has already promised to supply.

7. FINAL INSPECTION.

Building projects are incomplete without the approval of the building inspector. Their job is to make sure the product and the plan match the policy of the community. Take it to the next level. Your work and mine in the cause of God's Kingdom are always subject to God's final approval. And the big difference between a "Kingdom inspection" and a "bureaucracy inspection" can be summed up in one word—grace. "God is able to make all grace abound toward you, that you, always having all sufficiency in all things, may have an abundance for every good work" (2 Corinthians 9:8 NKJV). Grace in the process and grace in the completion. Grace to build a legacy that will bless others.

John Starr grew up in a tiny, 3-bedroom, 1-bathroom house with 9 other children. His bed was a mattress shared with his brother. His passion was to cheer a major league baseball team he could never afford to see in person. But he was taught manners and hard work. John's parents faithfully took the family to a church where a real estate agent by the name of Truett

Cathy attended. Cathy was his Sunday school teacher and was impressed by the boy's ethic and behavior.

He began to mentor John and found out more about the family. One week, he asked the boy to introduce him to his family. When they were introduced, Truett Cathy pulled a key from his pocket and handed it to the boy's father. The puzzled father listened as the future founder of Chick-fil-A explained, "This is a key to a house I own near here. It's a 7-bedroom house on four acres, fully paid for. I'd like to give it to you in an even swap for your house. When the astonished family went to sign the papers, Cathy handed them a $5,000 check for moving expenses.

John Starr is now a Chick-fil-A franchise operator, helping cash-strapped employees with such things as vehicles and paid vacations. He explains, "Truett lived a humble life. The more he made, the more he gave. Now it's my turn to pay it forward." [18] Truett Cathy's legacy lives on, in the lives he touched—and so will yours.

*"Giving money effectively is almost as hard as
earning it in the first place."*
– Bill Gates

CHAPTER 4

*From Generation to Generation:
The Wealth Transfer System*

You probably didn't know Luis Carlos de Noronha Cabral da Camara. But if you had, you could have been a lot better off financially. He was a wealthy aristocrat bachelor and resident of Lisbon, Portugal, whose story became a classic. He simply wanted to draw up a will. The problem? He didn't have family members or significant friends to name as beneficiaries.

So, Luis Carlos de Noronha Cabral da Camara picked up the Lisbon phone book and selected 70 names at random to receive a portion of his estate. When he died in the late 1980s, the 70 "beneficiaries" in his will were notified—and thought they were being scammed. Much to their delight, the call was legit and each "inherited" thousands of dollars.[19]

Thankfully, you have family and friends who can inherit your hard-earned wealth. And thankfully, there are systems already in place to make that transfer more significant than checking off names in a phone book.

INTERGENERATIONAL WEALTH

Transferring wealth to the next generations is predicted to be a powerful dynamic during the next four decades. Though dollar estimates vary, we can assume that trillions (with a T) of dollars will be transferred. Calling it a "Golden Age of philanthropy," a 2014 study by *Boston College Center on Wealth and Philanthropy* estimates that heirs will receive $36 trillion, federal taxes $5.6 trillion, and bequest to charities $6.3 trillion by 2061. Over the entire period from now to 2061 charity is expected to receive nearly $27 trillion, with $20 trillion of that amount by donors still living.[20] Paul G. Schervish, co-author of the report, later said his wealth and philanthropy estimates likely represented the "floor" rather than the "ceiling." Of course, not everyone agrees. Michael J. Weiss wrote in *Ad Age* that the "impending generational transfer of wealth in America may be more myth than reality because of a weak economy, sputtering stock market and faltering Social Security system." [21] And Russell N. James III penned a critique in the *American Review of Public Administration* called, "The Myth of the Coming Charitable Windfall," saying that estate gifts are largely offset by a reduction in current giving.[22] Where the numbers land is anyone's guess,

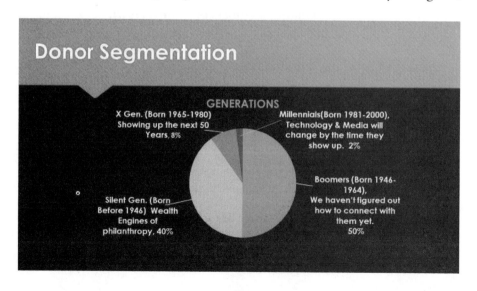

but The Great Handoff is a *fait accompli* for millions. And that begs the questions: "Where DID it go?" and "Where WILL it go in the future?" Of course, much of it went to and will continue to go to family members either named in an estate or assigned through probate. Still, an unknown percentage went elsewhere including to institutions and charities.

ORDER OR CHAOS

The intergenerational transfer of wealth will cause some stirs. Many people like to gift money while they are still alive. Yet we know that a great amount of wealth will be passed to children through an inheritance—some of it transferred in an organized, orderly way and some chaotically. Wealth transfer has generated—and will continue to—significant litigation. And the results will be noteworthy.

1. Higher divorce rates.
2. Declining marriage rates.
3. "Extended family" issues.
4. Family business holdings.
5. Family homes and property holdings.

Litigations aimed to prove disparities could divide both the estate and the beneficiary families. A survey by TD Wealth reflected on the prevalence of conflict, "According to a recent survey… nearly half (46 percent) of respondents identified family conflict as the biggest threat to estate planning in 2019, followed by market volatility (24 percent) and tax reform (14 percent) . . .. The survey also explored the various causes of family conflict when engaging in estate planning, citing the designation of beneficiaries (30 percent) as the most common cause of conflict. Other leading factors included not communicating the plan with family members (25 percent) and working with blended families (21 percent)." [23] Planned Giving will help to alleviate much of the controversy, but not all. The pie is only so large, and dividing its pieces evenly takes careful consideration. Whether those generations with pieces of the pie will be ready for their slice is up for grabs.

I like the story of the college student who took his father's advice and opened a checking account in a bank near the family home. A few weeks later the student called his dad in a panic. "Dad, that bank must be in trouble!" The father replied, "Trouble? Son, that's one of the most reliable institutions in the community. I just read its financial report and its growth rate is stellar." The son, still panicky said, "Well, you'd better check it again! Like I just got one of my checks back from them with a note that said, 'insufficient funds.' It must be running out of money!" Obviously, there was an education gap.

Back to the inheritance pie. I've often heard the question, "Should I give my children equal amounts in my estate?" My advice is to give each child what is fair based on their circumstances. If children have the same needs, then the inheritance could be split equally. I worked with one estate where the son was given more money during his lifetime and the mother took the added amount so the estate would be divided evenly among the sons. Oftentimes a child with special needs will be given a larger portion in the trust of the estate to care for living expenses and future medical needs. If a child contests the will because of an unequal share, a No-Contest clause can be added which states that any inheritor who contests the will forfeits any bequest. Hopefully, we will transfer wealth to adult children who have the wisdom to use it, otherwise we will damage them by subsidizing such behavior as addictions, laziness, and immorality.

RECESSION RECOVERY

The economy is usually more like riding in a raft on the Colorado River rapids than a paddlewheel boat ride on the Mississippi. So, there will be periodic ups and downs, such as in 2008. Giving to charity has increased in total dollars given. During 2018, more than $400 billion was given to charity, and nearly 69-70% of the giving came from individuals and families. But since 2008, the year of the Great Recession, donorship has been declining. The *Chronicle of Philanthropy* found that wealthier Americans gave less of their income to charities during the Recession. But from 2019-2030, US household assets are expected to increase from $87 trillion to $140 trillion, with $64 trillion of this amount in investable financial assets.

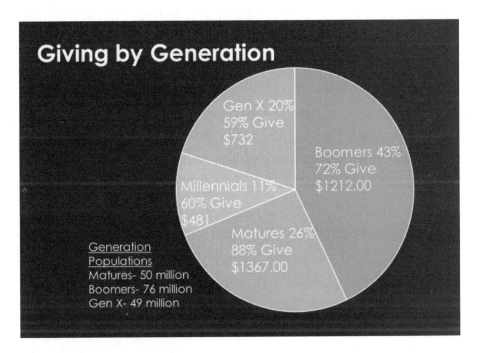

With Baby Boomers being viable donors for the next two decades, I suggest that they should remain a primary target for fundraising efforts. After 2030, Boomers' financial assets will begin to decline because of higher death rates. 2019 figures say that Boomer households now control 54% of total US households' net worth, while Millennials control only 4%. We also see that Boomers spend over $548 billion annually, about $300 billion more than Gen X. Boomers have collectively earned $3.7 trillion, more than twice as much as the $1.6 trillion the Silent Generation did at the same age. Boomers had the most assets to invest and therefore the greatest opportunity to benefit from the extended bull market after the crisis in the '80s. They are attracted to a balanced portfolio and income-generating investments like real estate (REIT's) and stocks that pay dividends.

ECHOES OF THE "BOOM!"

"Back in the day" is still a familiar phrase, but most would prefer the present—especially when you make comparisons. If the conditions were described accurately, most wouldn't want to "walk five miles to school with cardboard in their shoes." And an occasional restaurant outing might be preferred over the sameness of mom's canned food from the basement. Would you rather be among the 77% of Americans who own a cellphone or do you long for the days of party line phones with triple-digit phone numbers (and multiple neighbors listening in)? Which sounds more comfortable? Working from home or battling for lanes on the expressway at rush hour? On the job in a suit and tie or jeans and sneakers? I guess it is a matter of the good, the bad, or the ugly! But what is sure, cost of living is "alive and growing!" When I attended Ohio State University in 1966, tuition was $450 per year, and books would add an additional $200 per year. Now a year at a private institution will cost over $30,000 for room, board and tuition.

Blogger, Diana Arneson, gave a tongue-in-cheek overview of the Boomer years. "You will see a lot of baby boomers claim that they were always respectful to their elders, and never misbehaved like the kids of today. That's largely a crock. During the fifties and sixties, our parents and grandparents often complained that we were overindulged and poorly disciplined—the worst generation ever, in fact. And guess what? THEIR parents and grand-parents said the same thing about them." [24]

But when it comes to money matters, these days are better than the good old ones. Arthur Cheses, a high-net-worth research analyst with the research, analytics and consulting firm, Cerulli, estimates that $68 trillion will transfer during the next 25 years, and will be transferred by 45 million US households to their heirs and charities. He also estimates that most of those dollars will be transferred to Generation X. [25] The transfer of intergenerational wealth will come largely from the Baby Boomers and the Silent Generation, which makes it important to work across generational lines to realize all their giving potential.

In the next 10 to 15 years, the Silent Generation, which currently controls about $11 trillion of US assets, will share those assets through estate plans and bequests to younger generations. Overall net wealth is projected to grow by approximately $50 trillion during those years. But like a fading echo of one dynamite blast giving way to another, the boom may echo even louder within 25 years after the Gen Xers replace Boomers as the generation of greatest wealth. However, the future generations of retirees may change the giving landscape for many Christian organizations. Younger generations are less likely to give to religious or spiritual causes and more likely to give to animal rights and environmental and human rights causes.

As mentioned, parents and children find it awkward to discuss money, particularly when it involves estates and the issue of death. 68% of Millennials expect an inheritance, but only 40% of parents will probably leave one. Today the average net worth of Silent Generation retirees 70 years and older is $264,750, but since they are locked into lower mortgage rates on homes purchased in the '60s, they have less debt. Only 21% of children have been told how much they will receive. And there is a good chance that expectations could be out of line from what they will actually receive. Jay Zagorsky, a research scientist at Ohio State University, says one-third of inheritance recipients will "blow it." Time will tell, but we do know that 57% of workers have less than $25,000 in savings and investments, and a poll conducted by the Federal Reserve Board found that the average bequest to Baby Boomers was less than $50,000.

BEST- AND WORST-CASE SCENARIOS

According to the *Washington Post,* in wealthy families, only 10% give their children an understanding of how much they can expect. Eugene Lang who was called "an American folk hero," died at the age of 98. He had resolved not to leave his children a dime of his $50 million fortune while giving away $150 million and helping 16,000 students over the course of his lifetime. He felt his kids should fend for themselves. Lang said, "I gave them a good education and every encouragement to make it on their own. They should be able to stand tall." He didn't believe in luxuries and could be seen picking up a penny on the street. His son, Stephen said, "My father has a very healthy respect for what money can do but ultimately thinks it's quite a corrupting thing." Yet, inheritance cash can be put to very productive use by paying off high-interest debt. I always encourage heirs to put inheritance money in a separate account. If it becomes blended it is easy to spend.

The estimates of how much money Baby Boomers will inherit is all over the board. Best- and worst-case scenarios abound. Some speculate $10 trillion in the next 55 years, others $12 trillion over the next 20 years, while still others say $136 trillion over the next 55 years. Obviously, much depends on the strength of the economy, the stock market, and the viability of the Social Security system. Since 2001, stock market meltdowns have erased some $8 billion in shareholder wealth. Also, thanks to medical advancement and the emphasis on proper diet and exercise, Baby Boomers —and all Americans—are living longer: 78.87 years in 2019 and a projected 79.05 years in 2022.[26] So, Baby Boomers will have an extended retirement to fund. An interesting report by David Spiegelhalter for *BBC* provided a glimpse into life expectancy and population, "The UN estimates that the proportion of people over 60 will double between 2007 and 2050, as people will live longer, and lower fertility rates mean fewer young people. There will be two billion people over 60 in the world by 2050 and around 400 million over 80.[27] The Baby Boomer work years coincided with a period of robust economic growth during the 1960s. Home prices increased during the 1970s. And stock prices increased during the 1980s and 1990s. They are experiencing the most generous pensions in the nation's history.

TRAJECTORY

Researchers at Boston College calculated the sum of all US inheritances to be distributed within the next 50 years to be $41 trillion, based on modest growth of 2%. With current growth at 3% plus, it is estimated that the transfer might be as much as $136 trillion. Recently, BC analyst Paul G. Scherwich recalculated the math of the report and even considering economic recessions and stock market decreases, still holds to the figure of $41 trillion.[28] The bulk of the wealth transfer will go to 20% of Baby Boomers who will inherit $7.2 trillion from their parents. And the bigger transfer will be from Baby Boomers to their children.

RACE AND ETHNICITY FACTORS

Race and ethnicity figure into inheritance statistics. An analysis found that 23% of white Americans had already received an inheritance compared to 11% of black Americans. Hispanics received 4%. Despite large gains in income, minorities have not accumulated assets to pass on as bequests. During the last decade, black American median income rose 34%, while their median inheritance rose 12%. More than 50% of all black households with a member 70 years or older have no financial assets and nothing to bequeath. The Center for American Progress reports, "The average net worth of a white household was $919,000 in 2016. In contrast, the average net worth of a black household was just $139,000, showing a much larger difference of $780,000." [29] For Hispanics, the median income is $30,000. In many cases, the reason they have failed to accumulate monies for retirement may be that nearly half send money back to family in their country of origin. Of course, distributing monies as they earn it affects their retirement funds. Inheritance size is related to income. Bequests from Latinos and Asians averaged $94,000 and $76,100, compared to $55,100 for whites and $44,000 for blacks. Although there are few wealthy Latinos in the US, they are by far the most generous.

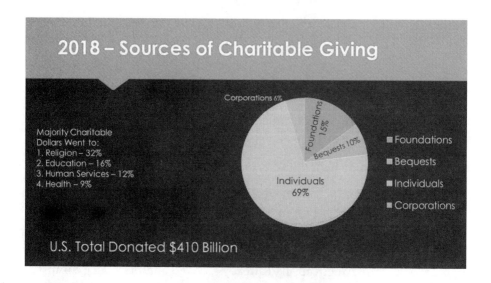

2018 – Sources of Charitable Giving

Corporations 6%

Foundations 15%

Bequests 10%

Individuals 69%

Majority Charitable Dollars Went to:
1. Religion – 32%
2. Education – 16%
3. Human Services – 12%
4. Health – 9%

- Foundations
- Bequests
- Individuals
- Corporations

U.S. Total Donated $410 Billion

CHARITIES AND WEALTH

Scherwich feels that of the $40 trillion transfer of wealth he projects, $6 trillion will go to charities. Silent Generation donors more often give money to churches and religious institutions. Boomers often are more inclined to "make a statement" by making donations for cultural needs that are still unmet. For example, Boomers are setting up foundations to support broad causes and education that aids domestic poverty, and some of those decisions can be to the detriment of their children and grandchildren.

For example, as a superintendent of schools, I always tried to attend extracurricular activities. One Saturday night I took my wife to a high school play presented by its drama department. As it progressed, I became very uncomfortable with the subject matter, and particularly the bedroom scenes. The following morning, I made a call to the high school principal and told him that I would be reviewing all future productions by the school's drama department and that I wanted to meet with the drama teacher.

After the meeting, I was informed that the teacher's union would be filing an unfair labor practice. Soon after that, the parent of one of the play's cast members expressed displeasure at my "interference" and asked to be included on the next board meeting agenda. At the meeting, she told the board that she felt the superintendent should be responsible for student education but not to establish the values and morals of the school district. The board members read the content of the play, and after she finished her position, affirmed that the superintendent has a responsibility in the development of values and morality of the school system.

Ten years later, I was serving as Vice President of Advancement at IWU. As I walked to my car after visiting a local manufacturer, I heard, "Mr. Munday, Mr. Munday!" A lady walked toward me, and as we met, she said, "You may not remember me, but I want to apologize to you. I am the lady who came to the school board meeting years ago to protest your actions. I was wrong in my effort to defend my daughter."

Of course, I accepted her apology and asked how her daughter was doing. She said her daughter was enrolled in a state college but had "ruined her life, with alcohol and drugs." Then she said sadly, "It has been a while since we have heard from her. It has been major stress to her father and me." I gave her a hug and told her that I would be praying for her daughter.

This is a common story of parents who in an effort to support their children, discredit the concept of morality. Chuck Colson said, "If we fail to recognize prevailing worldviews the worst that may happen is that we ourselves will be sucked into false thinking unaware – and lose our distinctive message."

Some of the funds that Boomers receive will come through trusts with strings attached. 20% of the Boomers are still paying college tuition for their own children. And more grandparents are establishing trusts for their grandchildren in plans such as a 529 college savings account which is exempt from federal taxes. Yet, Boomers can still be expected to include religious charities along with other causes:

> *"Never worry about numbers. Help one person at a time, and always start with the person nearest you."*
> –Mother Teresa

- 53% religious or spiritual

- 31% poverty relief

- 26% disaster relief

- 19% educational institutions

Charitable bequests exceeded $35 billion in 2017, which may be another pointer to the Great Intergenerational Wealth Transfer. People in the 65-79 age bracket are expected to transfer $10 trillion of the total wealth transfer to charity. Another encouraging factor to charities is that households with less than $1 million in wealth constitute 92% of the population and account for 50% of all lifetime charitable donations.

NET WORTH

The net worth of American families has risen by 40% over the last decade. For Boomers, well-paying jobs and homeownership were common after finishing college, while in contrast, it will take Millennials 19 years to save for a deposit on a home. (Only 1/3 of millennials own their own home compared to 2/3 of Baby Boomers at the same age.) It only took three years in the 1980s to save for a deposit on a home. Millennials spend 25% on housing, while Baby Boomers spend 6%. Boomers also pay $420 billion a year in federal income taxes and control 80% of US wealth.

ESTATE PLANNING PRIORITY

Planned giving is one of the best ways to leave a lasting legacy. The gift demonstrates which charities are most important to you and denotes to your family what charities were a big part of your life. It appears that 95% of the people have not included a charity in their planned giving. Even individuals that are well-off financially are hesitant to include a charity. They are afraid they or their family will fall on hard times. I hear this story repeatedly. Giving to a charity in wills or bequests alleviates the risks. The money doesn't go to that charity until the person's death. One study indicated that 54% of planned giving donors were from the Silent Generation or Baby Boomer generation. 44% of planned gifts were made by donors without children and 28% from bequests by donors with children.

Organizations and institutions MUST get involved in estate planning. Among the age 65 population, 30% are without a will, and 70% do not have a living will. Studies have found that 70% of the time family assets are lost from one generation to the next, and 90% of the time, assets are gone by the third generation. Organizations and fundraisers must put as much of their focus on the "receivers" of wealth as they do with the "givers." Someone said the economy must be getting stronger because 20 years ago it took two people to carry $10 worth of groceries; today one five-year-old can carry it. And if you notice, package size remains while package content has shrunk. And that former 25-cent hamburger that now costs $6 looks like it has been on a diet. Some of those "back-in-the-day" products and services give us a case of nostalgia.

Money is neutral, but people aren't. It can cause stress in relationships and is one of the leading causes of divorce. Individuals often *spend* a marriage into debt, which can lead to a marriage disaster. Yet $40 trillion will be passed to children despite the lack of household harmony. The question is "Will the transfer be in an organized orderly way or will it be chaotic?"

For the most part, planned giving will not only ready us for the retirement years, but it will also be our best method to distribute assets in a way that doesn't negatively impact family relationships. In the Great Handoff, it will also be used in distributing resources to organizations, charity, or to the government. Obviously, there is more benefit to giving during our lifetime. It brings a sense of contentment in seeing how our money is being spent. The 2017 *Wealth Transfer Report* shows that 61% of Americans surveyed planned to transfer ALL their assets upon death. Tony Martignetti wrote in *NonProfitPro* about ways wealth transfers can be made through a death beneficiary. "Your charity can receive a gift from any financial asset that has a death beneficiary feature. The most common example is life insurance." And then he adds, "Beyond life insurance, any of the following assets may have a death beneficiary, payable on death or transfer on death clause that can mean a long-term gift to your charity: 401(k) and 403(b) retirement plans; Individual Retirement Accounts — including Roth, traditional, Simplified Employee Pension and SIMPLE; commercial annuities; checking and savings accounts; and Brokerage accounts" [30]

We often have a difficult time releasing our assets. Someone wrote, "Between work and family, I'm really not spending enough quality time with my money." [31] Some think it's necessary to hold on to money for their own quality of life. But interestingly, nearly 1/4 of those surveyed felt they don't have enough funds to carry them to their death. Parents who make lifetime gifts get a chance to see how children are going to respond to the influx of new money and how they steward their wealth. Over the years most have witnessed children manage the money in a positive way while other children failed to adjust and wasted the funds.

Parents can learn from their process and adjust their wealth transfer if necessary. If parents give while they are living, they can resolve questions that emerge on the transfer of wealth. Children are also benefited by gaining a better understanding of how parents intended monies to be used.

- 29 is the average age for inheriting wealth from grandparents.

- 44 is the average age for inheriting wealth from parents.

SPENDING FROM INVESTMENTS

Since 40% of people die without a will, obviously older adults will spend from their investments, not their income. For example, if they had $10,000,000. in wealth and an income of $100,000., they might tithe on the $100,000, at $10,000. As charitable institutions, we must challenge people to give out of their *wealth* rather than their *income*. A tithe of the estate would be a much larger amount for a charity. For that reason, I have encouraged charities to ask for a tithe or a "child's portion" of the estate. This is a better way to establish a charitable legacy for your family.

GIVING OUT OF WEALTH

Why don't we who represent charities suggest giving out of wealth during their lifetime AND at death? Instead, we settle for advising the donor to give from their income only during their lifetime. Financial advisors need to be educated in this concept of giving out of income and wealth. Our older population is experiencing a larger number of deaths each year. This means that the transfer of wealth will continually increase. Most of the deaths are members of the Silent Generation, and this cycle will be followed by Baby Boomer deaths in less than a decade. Much of the wealth held by Baby Boomers are in tax-deferred retirements and may realize additional taxation levels on the assets' appreciated value. That's another reason to encourage this age group to make planned gifts.

Charitable bequests exceeded $35 billion in 2017, which again, points to a large intergenerational transfer of wealth. Will we be positioned for that transfer? Yes, if we present our nonprofits in the proper fashion. Wealthy people are often very charitable. Roper research's *Social Capital Community Benchmark Survey* (SCCBS) surveyed 30,000 people in over 40 communities. It revealed that in the US, people who give charitably make a lot more money than those who don't. It also showed that giving increased by 7% when people's wealth increased by 10%. They found that a family who gave away $100 more than another family in the same income bracket will earn an average $375 more as a result of their generosity. Giving increases happiness. [32]

Some of the richest people in the world donate billions every year, and their income doesn't seem to be diminishing. Bill Gates, perhaps the world's biggest philanthropist, has reportedly donated over $28 billion in his lifetime, yet his wealth keeps increasing year after year. He has been featured as #1 on the world's billionaires list more than anybody else, and he is worth an estimated $79.2 billion at the time of this writing. For the record, that's also the highest ever achieved on the Forbes' billionaire list. Warren Buffet's net worth was $44 billion in 2012 and he donated a massive $3.084 billion in the same year.[33]

VEHICLES OF TRANSFER

CPA Tim Cestnick identified 6 ways to transfer wealth to the next generation.

1. Intestacy laws.

2. Named beneficiaries on financial papers.

3. Joint ownership.

4. Trust.

5. Partnership or shareholder agreement.

6. Will.[34]

VALUES TRANSFER

A study by Bank of America's, *US Trust*, revealed that wealthy donors are guided by their personal values in their giving. "When determining which nonprofit organizations to support, the majority of high net worth individuals draw upon their personal values (74%), interest in the issue area addressed by the organization (57%) and having firsthand experience with the organization (54%).

"Donors don't give to institutions; they invest in ideas and people in whom they believe."

–G. T. Smith

Other factors include the reputation of the organization (50%) and the perceived need of the organization (49%)." [35] I am very concerned that we bequeath more than our material possessions, however. It is important that we teach and walk in a way that honors God and the values of His Word. I have witnessed many parents and families who practiced generosity and left that same spirit with their children. I am certain they had discussed the importance of generosity with their children.

Bruce and Dorothy exemplify that. They were godly people who left most of their estate to charity. On one occasion, I asked the children if they had any concern with the way their parents had distributed the estate. They answered, "No," and added, "We knew our parents loved the Lord and wanted the funds they were blessed with to be used to bless others. They set an example and our plans are to follow their lead with our own estates."

Another example is Hattie May Wiatt, who lived in the 1800s and is known for a 57-cent donation to her church. In that era, Sunday school was a rather new concept that began in the late 1700s as a way of educating children who worked in the factories all week. Christian philanthropists funded the venture, which also offered the children Christian teachings. It was so popular in Hattie's day that her classroom was filled to capacity—and Hattie was afraid to attend alone. Her pastor assured her that if the money could be raised the building would be enlarged and there would be room enough for everyone to attend. Hattie Wiatt died two years later, and her mother brought Hattie's little purse to the pastor. She explained, Hattie has been saving money to build a bigger church. When the pastor opened it there were 57 pennies inside. The pastor told his congregation about the 57-cent offering and auctioned the pennies off. $250 was raised, plus a Wiatt Mite Society was formed to raise more funds.

Hattie's 57 cents kept multiplying through donations, and soon enough funds had been given to purchase a house next to the church. It became the temporary site for the new classrooms of Hattie Wiatt's dream. Twenty-six years later, a follow-up report revealed the enormous results of Hattie's gift.

- The church now had over 2,000 in attendance.

- A hospital was built that treated thousands of patients.

- Temple University was organized in the classrooms.

A 57-cent investment passed along from a little girl's heart of concern has ministered to the needs of millions. What you may give or assist others in giving can be multiplied through planned giving. Organizations or ministries that lack space or funds, institutions of learning that need student scholarship money, and missionaries who need support partners can benefit along with you in the planned giving process. It is an opportunity too good to pass up that results in blessings too numerous to add up.

"God has given us two hands,
one to receive with and the other to give."
–Dr. Billy Graham

CHAPTER 5

The Generation Files

The words of Jesus are a template for living a life of service to others: "From everyone who has been given much, much will be demanded; and from the one who has been entrusted with much, much more will be asked" (Luke 24:40).

Even though the giving environment is increasingly unpredictable, the faithful efforts of organization fundraisers continue to have a payoff. *Giving USA* reports, "Amid a complex climate for charitable giving, American individuals, bequests, foundations, and corporations gave an estimated $427.71 billion to US charities in 2018." In the same report, Dr. Amir Pasic, Ph.D., the Eugene Tempel Dean of the Lilly Family School of Philanthropy, said, "Charitable giving is multidimensional, however, and it is challenging to disentangle the degree to which each factor may have had an impact. With many donors experiencing new circumstances for their giving, it may be some time before the philanthropic sector can more fully understand how donor behavior changed in response to these forces and timing." [36] "Disentangle" is apropos in discussing intergenerational wealth transfer. Each generation has a unique social and financial place in our culture. The Center for Generational Kinetics defines a generation, "A generation is a group of people born about the same time and raised around the same place. People in this "birth cohort" exhibit similar characteristics, preferences, and values over half their lifetime." [37] And each represents a unique view of values, money, and wealth that must be discovered. So, an overview of each might add insight into connecting with them. Let's look at five generations in a hypothetical breakfast setting for a glimpse into the life and times of people in each generation.

THE SILENT GENERATION:
BORN 1928 -1945 (73-90 YEARS OLD).

It is 1935. Meet Mr. & Mrs. Silents and their children. They rise early for a traditional breakfast of eggs, toast, fruit, oatmeal, milk, and coffee freshly brewed from an aluminum, stovetop coffee maker. The radio is on and the Glenn Miller Orchestra sets the tone for interspersed news reports, weather, family births or deaths, and updates about recovery efforts from the stock market crash. Mrs. Silents gets the children ready for school while Mr. Silents reads the newspaper and makes mental notes about making ends meet on his $1350 annual salary working on a government-funded construction site. Soon he's out the door and into his 1930 Ford Model T for a long workday. He thinks about the evening meal at the dinner table with his family and the Monopoly or Sorry board game that will be the evening's entertainment.

TOUGH TIMES.

The Silent Generation was preceded by the Greatest Generation, also known as the G.I. Generation and World War II generation, the demographic cohort following the Lost Generation. Demographers and researchers typically use the early 1900s as starting birth years and ending birth years in the mid to late 1920s, with 1901 to 1927 a widely accepted definition. They were shaped by the Great Depression and were the primary participants in World War II. [38] The Silents family household looks idyllic but that belies the fact that people of its generation were known as "Children of Crisis." The Silent Generation (aka, Matures) came of age under the shadow of the Great Depression, World War II, the Korean War, and the Cold War. Their attitudes toward life and work were formed in the crucible of economic upheaval, and America emerging as a superpower. They grew up in tough times, so they had a more constrained set of expectations. A 1951 TIME magazine article popularized the "Silent Generation" name, but described it as unimaginative, withdrawn, unadventurous and cautious because it always played by the rules. It was the only generation without an obvious "leader," but was self-motivated and secured more wealth than their elders. And because of their material wealth, the Silent Generation *still speaks* through resourcing others. Its cost of living dynamics:

- Average cost of a house: $3,600.

- Cost of gas: 15 cents.

- Average house rental cost: $40 per month.

- A bottle of Coke: 5 cents.

- Average price of a new car: $900.

- WWII model plane kits: 5 for $1.00.

The Silents family would buy its first house in the '60s with a low 3% mortgage rate and at midlife, experience a bull market in stocks and bonds. They would be able to retire after this period of high stock yield just before the crash hit. Between 1940-1960:

- The GNP-doubled.

- Real purchasing power increased by 30%.

- 80% of American families owned at least one car.

- Homeownership increased by 61%.

- Consumer debt rose from 22% in 1946 to 110% in 2002.

The Silent Generation believed that getting ahead was the result of hard work and diligence in the workplace. It knew what it was like to have lean times, so it was willing to work long grueling hours, and often took less than appealing jobs out of respect for authority, patriotism, and loyalty.

COMMON THEMES

- The Silent Generation was at its peak in the 1950s.

- It was the first generation smaller than the one that preceded it.

- It worked with the system and was not known for taking chances.

- It found jobs right out of school because the economy was booming after WWII.

- At the age of 30, its members were earning better wages and retired earlier than those who came before it.

- It was a smaller group because of the low birth rate during the 1930's—which put it in a better labor market.

- It gave leadership to the civil rights movement.

- It was the core of the "Silent Majority"—people who were usually silent about their opinion and public demonstrations.

DONOR DYNAMICS

The *Chronicle of Philanthropy* reported that 60% of the largest gifts made in 2015 were from donors over 70 years of age. During my years at Indiana Wesleyan University, nearly all of my major gifts (those of $100,000 or more) came from donors over 70; for example, $10.3 million from a 93-year-old and $6 million from a couple 79 and 77 respectively, $2 million from a 74-year-old, and $2 million from another couple, 92 and 93 respectively. AARP said, "Though fewer in number, the older Silent Generation remains a significant force in charitable giving, contributing an estimated $29 billion last year, an average of $1,235. That amounted to 20 percent of all charitable donations. [39] The Sharpe Group, a consulting and training organization that assists gift planning professionals, wrote, "Those 65 and over, currently comprised primarily of the Silent Generation, give more to charity and support more charities than any other generation. Older donors are also responsible for more noncash gifts—particularly gifts of appreciated securities—than any other age group. Regarding the oldest Americans:

> *The price of living is giving."*
> – Unknown

- They represent the vast majority of maturing planned gift revenues each year.

- The IRS indicates 92% of bequest dollars come from people who died at the age of 70 or older.

- 57% of bequest dollars are received from those dying between ages 70 and 89.

- 37% of bequest dollars are received from those dying age 90 and over.

- Estate plans that result in charitable distributions are typically executed late in life, mostly beyond the age of 75.[40]

BABY BOOMERS:
BORN 1946-1964 (54-72 YEARS OLD).

The ring of the wind-up alarm clock pushes the Boom family into a fine day in 1953. Soon, Mr. & Mrs. Boom and their children will be in their newly tiled kitchen sleepily consuming all or some of their Kellogg's Corn Flakes, a freshly thawed "Eggo" frozen waffle, and unfrozen orange juice concentrate. Mr. Boom pours coffee from the stainless-steel electric percolator and joins them in the new breakfast nook. Mrs. Boom hurries to get the children ready for school before she leaves for work as a TWA flight attendant. Mr. Boom scans the newspaper and watches Dave Garroway on the new "NBC Today" news show. Soon, he'll drive Mrs. Boom to the airport in their Chevy Bel Air and have another coffee in the breakroom at his $3,000 per year accounting job. That night, the family will gather in the living room to watch "Father Knows Best" on their console black and white TV.

BOOM!

"The cry of babies was heard across the land," historian Landon Jones described the births occurring in 1946. From 1954-1964, four million "Baby Boomers" were born. And echoes of that "BOOM!" still bounce off the walls of Main Street, Wall Street, and Madison Avenue. Suburban life evolved as Baby Boomers began moving to the outskirts of cities and built modest, mass-produced houses. The GI Bill helped with low-cost mortgages—and the advent of "family rooms." Boomers began opening credit card accounts to buy TVs, hi-fi systems, appliances, furniture, and new cars. *"American Bandstand"* and Walt Disney's *"Mickey Mouse Club"* kept them entertained. And Elvis Presley, Hula Hoops, Frisbees, and Barbie dolls topped their interest charts.

COMMON THEMES

- 10,000 Boomers turn 65 each day, and an estimated $59 trillion will be passed to Millennials and their heirs. Without planning this could be subjected to significant taxes.

- Boomers comprise 28% of the population.

- Boomers are responsible for over half of consumer spending.

- Boomers control 80% of personal financial assets.

- 1 of 3 Boomers relies on Social Security benefits alone.

- 75% of Boomers claim benefits when they turn 62 out of financial necessity.

- Boomers face uncertain Social Security benefits (In 1950, 16 workers paid for each retiree's SS benefits; in 2010, 3.3 workers paid for those benefits; In 2025, a projected 2 workers will pay for each retiree's benefits).

By 2030, when all Baby Boomers are on Social Security, entitlements will consume 61 cents of every federal dollar, starving out other neglected investments—and with a less-skilled workforce, lower rates of job creation, and an outdated infrastructure.

- Boomers enjoy a higher quality of life and want maximum healthcare coverage.

- Boomers want their kids to grow up with the same middle-class values as theirs.

DONOR DYNAMICS

Boomers were born into times of prosperity and economic expansion. Feeling they *deserved* these riches and opportunities, they developed their own "Me Generation" sense of entitlement. Yet, 58% of baby boomers aren't even confident in their children's ability to properly use their inheritance. A study by *US trust* says that only half of millionaire Baby Boomers think it's important to leave money to their children. One-third said they would rather leave it to charity rather than their children. Boomers would approve of Warren Buffet's comment that he wants to leave his kids enough to *do anything* they want, but not so much that they can *do nothing*. Accordingly, many Boomers have raised children who are unequipped to inherit large amounts of money and wealth. Having been given most of what they want since childhood, they have followed their parents' model of generous spending.

It reminds me of the story about a wealthy businessman who was stopped near the entrance of his office building by a man who said, "Sir, you probably don't remember me, but 10 years ago—on this very spot—I asked you for twenty dollars and you gave it to me. You'll never know what that did for me!" The building owner said humorously, "I don't remember that, but I suppose you've come to pay me back and give me the inspiring story." The man looked rather sheepish and said, "Well, not exactly; I was wondering if you might have an extra twenty on you."

MAJOR RESOURCE

Baby Boomers are and will continue to be a major resource for intergenerational wealth transfer. For the next two decades, it will be the most important segment of a fundraiser's donor base. Although many have experienced divorce and are living in a blended family situation, many Boomers will have funds remaining at their death to pass to charitable causes. *U.S.*

News and World Report study said, "Controlling 70% of all disposable income in the U. S., Boomers are a dominant financial force in the marketplace." [41] As mentioned, the Great Intergenerational Wealth transfer may be in the range of $18 trillion, $35 trillion, $44 trillion, or $68 trillion. No matter the figure you use there will be large amounts of money. And in planning your appeal to Boomers, you might want to consider these tips:

- Use images – use media to tell the story of how they can change the world through your organization.

- Appeal to their emotions – they give because the message has reached their heart, rather than because of facts and statistics. They want to know that their giving will give hope.

- Tell stories – tell how their giving can change the world, not about the awesomeness of your organization.

GENERATION X:
BORN 1965-1980 (38-53 YEARS OLD).

It is a rainy day in 1970, so the snooze button on the alarm clock has taken a beating but finally wins, and Mr. & Mrs. Gentry are followed by their children to the kitchen. The breakfast menu will include Froot Loops and milk, Tang, egg muffin sandwiches, and coffee brewed in a white Proctor Silex coffee maker. Mrs. Gentry will fix sandwiches and put them in a Barbie or Disney lunch box, while Mr. Gentry checks his Day-Timer for calendar appointments. Soon he'll be in his new Oldsmobile 442 muscle car on the way to an $8,000 per year job as a computer programmer. Mrs. Gentry will drive their VW to her $5,000 per year accounting job at the J. C. Penny store in the new mall.

Forward to the present, and Generation Xers are entering the most financially rewarding stage of their lifetime. With increased income and savings, they will experience the highest increase in the share of national wealth—going from 14% to 31% in 2030, a net worth of $22 trillion.

COMMON THEMES

- Gen X is still recovering from the 2008 economic downturn and is still struggling with student loans.

- Gen X and Millennials tend to support global and environmental causes rather than local and traditional causes.

- Gen X will be inclined to support issues and values different than other generations, such as climate change and LGBTQ rights.

- Gen X struggles with addictions, moral laxity, and materialism.

- Gen X has been buffeted by tumultuous political and economic conditions. It is uncertain about America's position in the world and even about its own place in America.

- Contrary to media, Gen X is a savvy generation, willing and able to take on the challenges they face.

This generation was the last to taste the fruits of a postwar economy and the first not to need their parents' wealth or success. Unlike generations before, its work is "just a job," and employment options abound. So, deserving or not, it has been dubbed a "slacker" generation. Independent, self-sufficient, and sometimes totally forgotten, it is a generation with values as diverse as the culture in which it lived.

INDEPENDENT AND SELF-SUFFICIENT

The prevalence of divorce threatened the traditional family. Single parent homes emerged. Adding to its social unease, single parents began to rely on the latch-key system, where children let themselves into their home after school while mom was working. "Computer parenting" characterized its lone afternoons—making it ("virtually") more independent and self-sufficient. Children saw hardworking parents suffer burnout in the corporate world, causing them to become very entrepreneurial—and enjoying working independently, without supervision. Yet in the workplace, they were very social, enjoying their workplace camaraderie, while making independent choices as needed.

Contrarily, for many Gen Xers, hard work is a pragmatic necessity and they were careful in planning for the future. In many ways, they embraced the values of the Matures. Adam Vaccaro wrote in *Inc.*, "Whereas Boomers have been notorious for 'self-esteem parenting,' Gen Xers seem to be returning to the more authoritative parenting style. They know the world is dangerous, and they're not about to let their kids move as freely as Boomer parents have." [42] Since they have lived through uncertain formative years, Gen Xers seem to deal better with economic ups and downs than the Boomers.

DONOR DYNAMICS

Gen Xers are sandwiched between the rising costs of healthcare for their aging parents and the rising cost of educating their own children. Those concerns overshadow everything, including their retirement plans. In addition, nearly 50% of this generation reportedly lost half their wealth between 2007 and 2010 in the housing and financial collapse of the Great Recession. Their average net worth dropped by 45% as compared to the Boomers' 25-28% dip. Gen X used credit cards to survive and a study by Allianz Life Insurance indicates that it carries more debt than any previous generation. But Gen X is more willing to take risks, and those risks paid off. Richard Fry wrote in a Pew Research Center Think Tank report, "While the economic downturn had a disproportionately negative impact on Gen Xers, their fortunes have rebounded more than those of other generations during the post-recession economic expansion and as home and stock prices have risen. Since 2010, the median net worth of Gen X households has risen 115%. [43]

MILLENNIALS:
BORN 1981-1996 (22-37 YEARS OLD).

On a hazy morning in 1980, Mr. Miller walks in the door after a morning jog for a breakfast of egg white omelet, oat bran muffin, and sugar-free orange juice. He gets his second mug of decaf from his Mr. Coffee while Mrs. Miller drinks the last of a diet shake and watches "Good Morning America." Soon the Millers jump into their new Ford F-Series truck and make their way to their combined $24,000-a-year data entry jobs. On the way home, they discuss last week's episode of "Dallas" and plan to watch the next episode that evening.

MIXED BAG

Millennials are now the biggest generation. Some view them as confident, open-minded, and ambitious—but also narcissistic, distrustful and anxious. Their parents overemphasized self-esteem and being happy while they became absorbed in a culture of diversity, decentralized authority and reality TV. They became the most closely supervised generation in American history, which may have been a reaction to the independence observed in children of Gen X. They were influenced by their relationships with the Internet. A sense of insecurity was present after they experienced 9/11 and mass shootings. Millennials like to give to charities that make the world a better place to live and care less about how their money is spent. Financially bold, they are the least hesitant to invest in the stock market. Yet, Millennials between 25- and 34 still carry an average debt of $42,000. Only 23%

of Millennials say the stock market is the best place to put money during the next decades.

Observances of the Millennials are a mixed bag. While some call them a caring generation, others decry that. Research by Dr. Jean Twenge concludes that the notion of Millennials being more caring, community-oriented, and politically involved than previous generations "is largely incorrect." She quotes Christian Smith: "The idea that today's emerging adults are a generation leading a new wave of renewal civic-mindedness and political involvement is sheer fiction." [44]

BIBLICAL WORLDVIEW

Other gaps emerge, the largest being between the beliefs of older adults and those of Millennials relating to the nature of God, the existence of absolute moral truth, concepts concerning evil, and the personal importance of faith. Millennials are the least religious generation in US history; 1 of 4 is unaffiliated with any religion. They are raising a new set of challenges to Christianity and to the US, whose morals and value systems have long reflected Biblical principles. But they are a generation least likely to possess a biblical worldview. Religious pollster, George Barna, estimates that just 4% of Millennials have a biblical worldview. Their lifestyle is indicative:

- 18% of adults over 30 claim an atheist-agnostic faith preference, while 28%of Millennials claim this category.

- Nearly 2/3 support same-sex marriage.

- 44% prefer socialism over capitalism.

- 15% claim to be part of an LGBT community

The *Worldview Measurement Project* included 20 questions related to Biblical behavior. Millennials were statistically different from other adults on 14 indicators. Differences of 15% points or more were the moral acceptability of cheating on taxes, using non-prescription drugs for recreation purposes, same-sex marriage, and being less likely to worship God other than within a church service. 60% of Millennials say that Christianity is judgmental and 64% say that "anti-gay" best describes most churches today. It has been reported that among youth raised in some degree of "Christian" homes, 3/4 will change or desert that faith after high school. If parents play a major role in their children adopting a Christian worldview (and I believe they do!) the Millennials with their low biblical view will pass to their children an even lower reason to acquire a Christian worldview. And Short of a major revival, today's churches will need an attempt to intervene and reach the next generation with the Gospel message. Therefore, unless something radical takes place in our society, the millennial generation will likely never reach 10% who have a biblical worldview.

COMMON THEMES

- Millennials are less prejudiced than previous generations.

- Millennials are more focused on their own interests rather than outside interests.

- Millennials enjoy eating out with friends but are more spontaneous and adventurous in their cuisine.

- Millennials have lower earning rates, resulting in having fewer money reserves and fewer assets than their parents. They also are more likely to have less money in the bank—less than $1,000 in savings.

- Along with paying off student loans and paying high rent, Millennials are slower to buy a home.

- Millennials spend their money on convenience services like Uber, BNB, Grubhub, and they favor gadgets, designer clothes, Starbucks, live entertainment, and sports events. 46% of Millennials made impulse purchases because "they just got paid." 68% of females and 61% of males are susceptible to impulse purchases because of sales and discounts.

- Millennials are putting off marriage. From 1970-2012, the US marriage rate dropped by 60%. Single-parent homes, same-sex marriages, and adults choosing not to have children contribute to the creation of a new family structure. Pew Research reports average wedding costs are going higher and may be a factor for Millennials waiting longer – average wedding costs may range from $20,000 to $75,000 depending on your location in the nation. A career, self-fulfillment and financial security are more important than marriage or starting a family. In 2017, the 787,251 divorces were the lowest since 1968.

Pew Research also found that 39% of Americans who have been married since 2010 are married to someone of a different faith. The most common age of divorce is 30 years of age, and 42- 45% of first marriages end in divorce; 60% of second marriages end in divorce, and 73% of third marriages end in divorce.

- Millennials consider their use of technology as having allowed them a better work-home balance than their parents.

- Millennials have a strong sense of individualism which leads to the use of "I" and "me" more often than past generations.

- 24 of 25 Millennials don't have a biblical worldview.

Millennials also want work that provides for flexibility and more vacation time. But unlike previous generations, work does not "possess" their lives. Some speculate that the increased use of screen-time makes them less happy and more depressed—leading to more self-harm and suicide attempts.

DONOR DYNAMICS

Millennials believe that wealth is defined by the way you live more than by the amount of money you possess. They define success by doing meaningful work and spending money on rare experiences. 20% of young Millennials said they are unable to save, and most do not operate on a budget, largely because their parents never taught them how to budget or save. So, 20% of Millennials are reliant on their parents into their 30's.

Many parents who have provided the federal tax allowance, $15,000 per year, to their children, have given it as a gift, but the extra money has been used to enhance Millennial lifestyles—more discretionary spending, such as a nicer car or home remodeling, rather than spending for household stability. Since that money was a gift, parents feel that they do not have the responsibility to interfere in the way their Millennial children spend it. As a result, the parents make the children dependent on the annual gift and contribute to their financial delinquency. Instead of the children choosing more financial stability, they chose to increase their lifestyle. Millennial trends are indicators of their donor potential.

- The purchasing power of Millennials is estimated to be $170 billion per year.

- Millennials often engage with causes to help other people, not institutions.

- Millennials support issues rather than organizations.

- Millennials prefer to perform smaller actions before fully committing to a greater cause.

- Millennials are influenced by the decisions and behaviors of their peers.

- Millennials treat all their assets (time, money, network, etc.) as having equal value.

- Millennials need to experience an organization's work without having to be on site.

TOO LATE?

With the increase in life expectancy, wealth is increasingly transferred to the next generation too late to have a major impact. Previous generations have already paid off their mortgage and their children are completing their education. Most feel the money would have served a better purpose a decade before. Another option would have been for the parents to give the inheritance to their children early, not knowing their own retirement needs. This points to the importance of a gifting strategy before retirement. Giving money to adult children or grandchildren early also carries a risk.

> *"Feeling gratitude and not expressing it is like wrapping a gift and not giving it."*
> – William Arthur Ward

Do they know the value of money and the hard work that is represented by the money designated for retirement?

POST-MILLENNIALS (GEN Y-Z):
BORN 1997-2012 (6 -21 YEARS OLD).

At 7 a.m. this Monday in the year 2000, a cellphone alarm buzzes as the cellphone wiggles across the nightstand. Scott Post was glad he heard it. He had forgotten to un-mute it after last night's "U2" concert. He checks his text messages, quickly showers, and then looks at his email. Then, realizing the lost time, Scott grabs a slice of cold pizza and a can of Red Bull as he heads out the door. Jumping into his Jeep Cherokee, he fastens his seatbelt and chooses a song from his iPod playlist. But as the "Friends" theme song is playing, he can almost smell the aroma of that missed cup of espresso. He shows his ID to security and rushes to his office at his $35,000 per year software engineer job.

GEN Y OR Z

Scott is a "Post Millennial," otherwise known as Gen Y or Gen Z, depending on the age. The Center for Generational Kinetics reported, "The end of the Millennial generation and the start of Gen Z in the United States are closely tied to September 11, 2001. That day marks the number-one generation-defining moment for Millennials. Members of Gen Z—born in 1996 and after—cannot process the significance of 9/11 and it's always been a part of history for them." [45] Anne Gherini, marketing head for *Inc.,* wrote, "Over the past decades, Millennials have taken much of the limelight and have been a primary focus of sales and marketing teams. Times are changing. Gen-Z is finally taking the spotlight from its more well-known predecessors… According to research from *Bloomberg*, Gen-Z will surpass Millennials in 2019 as the most populous generation, comprising roughly 32 percent of the population." [46] Classy.org also described them, "Gen Z, also known as 'Philanthroteens,' refers to a cohort of young people born in the late 1990s and later. As of 2017, they make up 27 percent of the world population and account for 2 billion people. Moreover, by the year 2020, the number is expected to rise to 2.6 billion individuals" [47]

COMMON THEMES

Post Millennials (Generation Y and Z) is the latest and least known of the generation cohorts. But they are making social and financial tracks that will be worth following. Wikipedia offers additional insights on Generation Z:

- The Great Recession taught Generation Z to be independent, leading it to an entrepreneurial desire—especially after seeing their parents and older siblings struggle in the workforce.

- Gen Z is faced with a growing income gap and a shrinking middle-class, which has led to increased stress levels in families.

- Church attendance during young adulthood was 41% among Generation Z, compared to 18% for Millennials, 21% of Generation X, and 26% for Boomers, when they were at the same age

- Gen Z is the most diverse generation to date, many identifying with multiple ethnic or racial identities.

- Gen Z challenges what is expected of them, both in their personal and public lives.

- Generation Z tends to be highly creative.

- While Gen Z values education, their personal brand is seen as more important.

- Generation Z is more conservative, more money-oriented, more entrepreneurial, and more pragmatic about money compared with Millennials.

- Generation Z is the first cohort to have Internet technology readily available at a young age. The use of social media has become integrated into their daily lives and used primarily to keep in contact with friends and family.[48]

DONOR DYNAMICS

Alice Berg described members of Generation Z statistically, "By 2020:

- They'll make up 40% of all customers.

- 26% of those 16-19 will volunteer.

- 60% want their work to make a difference.

- 76% are worried about the planet.

- 30% have already donated to an organization.

- 1 in 10 wants to start a charity.

- They will prefer mobile apps to give." [49]

- The author also gave insight into Post Millennial donor trends:

- 57 percent of young people will save their money rather than spend it.

- 32 percent of Gen Z donate their own money.

- 26 percent of 16 to 19-year-olds practice volunteering on a regular basis.

- 50 percent are looking for a job in volunteering.

- 10 percent want to start their own nonprofit organization. [50]

Emily Anatole wrote in *Forbes* online, "Whereas Gen Ys (ages 18-34) are optimistic, Gen Zs are realistic. They understand how scary the world can be, having grown up post 9/11, in the wake of the Great Recession and amid countless reports of school violence. They've seen the effects of the economy firsthand and are more aware of troubling times. These dark events will undoubtedly make them more cautious and security-minded but will also inspire them to improve the world.[51]

Yet, the younger the generation, the more post-Christian they seemingly become. George Barna said, "Momentum is currently on the side of unabashedly embracing postmodern morality." He adds, "we are moving steadily toward moral anarchy." [52] Ken Ham and Britt Beemer wrote, "Church youth already are *lost* in their hearts and minds in elementary, middle and high school not in college as many assume." But God still calls generations to Himself. A friend told me of his Gen Z granddaughter standing alone in the rain beside the flagpole of her middle school, praying for its students and administrators on the annual "See You At the Pole" prayer day. Her father founded a national prayer organization called "Never the Same." The objective of its "Claim Your Campus" arm is to see 1 million students pledge to pray IN their schools, FOR their schools. Over 30,000 students have already signed on and meet in weekly prayer groups across the nation.

So, all is not lost until those who follow Christ and His Word, have ceased to seek the lost.

"If you have accomplished all that you have planned
for yourself, you have not planned enough."
– Edward Everett Hale

CHAPTER 6

The Priority of Planned Giving

Planned giving will be an integral part of The Great Handoff. Donors are willing to pass on to us the results of their hard work in exchange for the opportunity to make the world a better place. Almost everyone qualifies for a planned gift. Studies say 70% of the time, family assets are lost from one generation to the next, and assets are lost 90% of the time by the third generation. Obviously, both families and their charities must be concerned with planned giving—an orderly transfer of assets from one generation to the next. Who are the best prospects for planned giving? We know that personal interests change as we get older. The same is true with our charitable interests. Charitable causes that I felt were important at age 35-40 are no longer my priorities. My life experiences have influenced and captivated my interests. Let's look at the profile of a person who qualifies as a planned giving prospect.

First and most important, the donor has been a regular donor to your charity. Their consistent donations signify a strong relationship with them.

I have always said that consistency in giving is more important than the size of the gift. For that reason, I develop a spreadsheet of donors that indicates their giving for the past five years. If the donor has given for several years, it indicates that they appreciate and have a relationship with my charitable organization.

Second, planned giving prospects are generally older. They are thinking about estate planning options as they get older and determining what should be done with their assets. In terms of the time value of money, we know that older people will die sooner, and their planned gift will be realized by the charity in a shorter period. Think of it this way. A person 40 years old decides to give your charity a gift of $50,000 as a bequest. Under normal circumstances, your charity will not receive that gift for another 40-50 years, while a 70-year-old person's similar bequest may be realized in 10-20 years.

Third, the prospect does not have family or heirs to which they can leave their estate.

Fourth, almost every prospect for planned giving has assets, whether a home or a life insurance policy. Charitable gifts made during a person's life are almost always more tax-efficient than gifts made at death because they have the potential of benefits from both the income and estate tax deductions. This is another reason for all adults to consider planned giving.

Although we focus on our larger donors in a capital campaign, a planned giving strategy should be more widespread and focused on all donors large and small. The average size of a planned gift in the US is $35,000 to $75,000. It also is important that we focus on women in planned giving. When I started fundraising 30 years ago, the preponderance of my calls was made on men, however, as fellow Boomer Bob Dylan wrote, "The times they are a changin'." Currently, 64% of all donations are made by women—and further, women make 84% of all philanthropic decisions.

I am sure part of the percentage is their longer lifespan. After the male spouse passes, the female spouse usually makes the estate decisions. We do know that women are widowed in 80% of all marriages. And it should be noted that women are more altruistic in their giving. They give a larger percentage than their male counterparts (3.2% compared to 1.9%). We also know that women have a greater tendency in retirement to give back and that women derive more happiness in helping others than they do in spending on themselves.

While the "annual fund" only gives you a projection for the year based on cash donations or pledges, planned giving enables you to make longer-range plans. Planned giving is a sizable donation given over time, or as part of a donor's estate. Planned gifts are often 200-300 times the size of annual gifts. With many not-for-profits, it is the difference between surviving and thriving.

SIMPLICITY AND FLEXIBILITY

We work with a wide range of ages (50-90 years) in the audience when we are talking planned giving—but some have been left out of the conversation. Because of financial stewardship concerns, some charities only mail to donors 65 years-old and older. While some studies show that the average age at which donors make a will to include charitable causes is 79, other research indicates that 43% of individuals who include a charity in their will are under the age of 55 years old.

What we know for sure is that donors who make a planned gift also increase their annual support to that charity. Dr. Russell James, The CH Foundation Chair of Personal Financial Planning professor, found that donors who included a charity in their estate plans give more to the annual fund ($3,171 per year) *after* they include the charity. Penelope Burk in her best-selling book, *Donor-Centered Leadership,* reflected that even though bequests accounted for $23.4 billion of giving in 2012, that number could have been increased substantially if fundraisers had actively approached *everyone* who was willing to leave money to charity when they die. I think she is right. Those of us in the charity world are failing to make the contacts. We have allowed charities to think that planned giving is a complex, legal operation that requires much expertise and expense. Consequently, many charities fear it will consume too much of their annual budgets with attorney fees, etc. But it just isn't that bulky; it operates similar to an annual fund: Identify the donor, cultivate the donor, and ask the donor for a planned gift. According to *Giving USA*, individuals make up 71% of the charitable giving in the US. But only 10% of Americans utilize planned giving. Why? We have failed to make the Ask or haven't developed relationships with potential donors.

VITAL TOOL

"Planned gifts are only for the wealthy" is a misconception many nonprofits have accepted as fact. Do you consider yourself wealthy? Most of us do not. I remember a few years ago when I made regular calls on two very precious ladies who at the age of 90 were working every day on their 100-acre farm. They wore the same dresses and aprons almost every time I called on them. You would have thought they had barely enough money to buy food, as neither would hit the scales at more than 100 pounds. An old stove in the middle of one room in their house provided heat for the winter. On one occasion, I inquired how they wanted to use the farmland after they passed and was surprised to find that they had not yet made that decision. But they both felt that their mother would want the money spent on providing nursing scholarships. I shared with them that nursing was one of IWU's largest majors and that we had students who needed financial help in that area. We arranged for them to take a tour through our nursing department and suggested that we could recognize their mother with a picture display.

Within a few weeks, they were eager to consider supporting the nursing program. At the ages of 93 and 94, both ladies passed and the IWU nursing program received $1.3 million. Over one million dollars from two elderly ladies who considered themselves "poor" and lived a very simple lifestyle blessed the University with a nursing scholarship fund that continues to provide for students in need! The ladies had never made a gift to the annual fund, probably because they felt they could not afford it.

Planned giving is a vital tool to help charities reach and supplement their budget goals. To your donors, it is more than just giving money, it allows them to become its beneficiaries—along with their causes. In my opinion, it is a WIN-WIN giving opportunity! Why are fewer Americans not giving to charity, even though overall giving has been increasing since the Great Recession?

> *"Wealth is not to feed our egos, but to feed the hungry and to help people help themselves."*
> – Andrew Carnegie

Wealthy donors are filling the gap, but we also need to help middle-income donors see the need to make a gift—no matter how small. In 2015, only 24% of taxpayers reported a charitable gift. Economists conclude that the number of households making room in their budget for charitable gifts is shrinking.

GIVING HABITS

Some speculate that Americans have fallen out of the habit of giving, so charities have become reliant on the support of the more affluent—which now accounts for 75% of all itemized giving. Herzog and Price identified four types of givers.

1. *Impulsive givers* – 40 percent of givers who respond to an immediate need a sustained practice of giving to charities.

2. *Planned givers* – 16 percent of givers who have thoughtful and specific giving objectives and organized giving routines that include giving (often automatically) to charities.

3. *Habitual givers* – 6 percent of givers who give to charities out of a habit of giving, but do not give much thought to their donations.

4. *Selective givers* – 17 percent of givers who may give to charities consciously but lack ongoing giving routines.

I feel that many Christian charities have become dependent on larger gifts at the expense of cultivating the "Habitual" or "Selective" donors. Cultivating donors at any level takes time and effort—and every donation is important. Admittedly, running an annual fundraising event is hard work! I recall the many hours I spent setting up golf tournaments, banquets, "telesales," etc. But it was through those experiences that I developed relationships that not only spurred their giving but caused them to make even larger gifts later as part of a planned gift.

GIVER'S CHOICE

Donor Advised Funds (DAF) are growing in popularity. DAF's are one of the fastest-growing charitable vehicles used. There are more than 700,000 individual DAF accounts in the US. They have doubled in size during the past five years and collectively hold more than $121 billion, all of which are destined for charities. DAF donors recommended over $19 billion in grants to qualified charities. *DonorPerfect* lists five main advantages:

- *Recommend grants to their favorite charities and causes* - DAF charities pay out more than 20 percent of their assets each year? Compare that to the five percent that private foundations payout annually.

- *Streamline their giving* - DAFs alleviate administrative burdens like recordkeeping, and often offer advanced features like reporting that traditional "checkbook philanthropy" can't.

- *Establish a charitable legacy* - DAF donors often have the opportunity to create a succession plan for their DAF, effectively advising what happens to the DAF after their lifetime.

- *Involve their family in philanthropy* - DAFs offer multiple entry points for the next generation to be involved in philanthropy.

- *Donate complex assets* - Donors are looking beyond their checking accounts to realize that their non-cash assets, like privately held stock, cryptocurrency or tangible property, can be donated to charity. [53] The Crawford Heritage Community Foundation includes a sample bequest form on their website:

> *I give, devise and bequeath_____*
> *[Describe dollar amount, property to be given, or proportion of your residuary estate] to the Crawford Heritage Community Foundation, EIN #25-1813245, a not-for-profit corporation located in Meadville, Pennsylvania, 16335, to be added to the [insert name of fund currently managed by the community foundation]*
> *_____ Fund, a component fund of the Crawford Heritage Community Foundation, and I direct that this bequest become part of this Fund.* [54]

The actual number of DAFs in the United States is now 728,563. This total should surpass one million in 2020. People who criticize DAF's for not distributing the money immediately may be unaware that less than one percent remains dormant. The fact that they give anonymously only occurs in about one percent of the DAF donations. DAF's offer intergenerational wealth transfer opportunities since they have built-in succession plans, a Successor Advisor is appointed to assume the responsibility of the Primary Advisor of the DAF. This feature allows the family to continue donations to the charity their parents loved and appreciated. A further advantage of the DAF is that a donor can outsource the transfer process of unusual assets such as privately held stock or property.

A donor can make a charitable contribution of cash, stock, or property and receive an immediate tax deduction. The donor is not required to distribute the money in the year it is given, and the money invested can grow tax-free. However, the DAF requires an initial gift of $5,000 or more (but may be added to in increments as low as $500). Other opponents of the DAF are concerned that donated funds do not go directly to the charity and that the DAF becomes a holding tank for charitable donations. Money is placed in the "tank" and allowed to grow until the donor decides which charities they wish to support. But charities usually need the funds now! Foundations, on the other hand, tend to be more expensive to start with more time in administering. A foundation is required by law to distribute 5% of their net asset investments on an annual basis while the DAF is not required to distribute on an annual basis—but distributes more than 20% of their money on an annual basis. My greatest concern is that the DAF protects the identity of the donor, preventing the charity from knowing who made the contribution (to properly thank them or cultivate the donor for a future gift). Also, by not sharing that they have included a charity as a bequest, the charity cannot follow their receipting protocol. We know that for everyone who notifies a charity of a bequest—7 to 8 donors will not give notice.

No one should *have* to give to charity. It is a choice based on one's values and generosity. But too often that generosity is without guidelines. Many donors do not know how much they *should* give. Our job is to provide donors with charity and giving information, giving standards, and giving expectations. Some accumulate and hold on to wealth out of fear that at some time, they may not have enough. According to *Psychtimes,* giving has its own phobia: Peniaphobia (fear of poverty). Sufferers become so fearful of losing money they are unable to enjoy life in the present moment. Consequently, some will be generous in death but not while they are living—and others will never be generous. Philanthropy is cheapened when donors fail to give at the appropriate level based on their assets. Only 9-10% of people say they have put bequests in their wills, but 30% say they would if asked. We must *Ask* for planned gifts.

MULTIPLE PLANS

Again, planned giving isn't as difficult as some might believe. Basically, it is a three-step process for organizations and fundraisers.

- First, *identifying* prospective donors.

- Second, *cultivating* those donors through building a relationship with them.

- Third, *asking* them for a specific gift.

Planned giving offers several ways for the donor to respond, including bequests, annuities, charitable trusts, life insurance, assets from retirement plans, property, or collectibles. This allows the donor a great deal of flexibility. However, in my opinion, the easiest to ask for and the least complicated to administer are:

- Wills (Bequests)

- Annuities

- Charitable Remainder Trusts

- Appreciated Stock

MOVING UP

The average time for planned gifts to grow from inception to maturity is 7-10 years. Many charities think that elongates the giving process when they need the money *now*. Planned giving is a people process. During my 20-year tenure as VP for Advancement at IWU, 90% of planned gifts were given by individuals 60-82 years of age. And we all know that people give to people. Similar to asking for an annual gift, the details of the mechanical process can be executed through consulting an attorney or advisor later. People who believe in your charity and give through their will generally increase their giving to the annual fund. They become part of the database, moving up in their giving each year, and making the larger planned and major gift. Are Americans volunteering and giving to charity less each year? Sadly, the answer is "yes." It may be that the giving habit was broken by the Great Recession of 2008. And people are now concerned with a sustained source of income since their house is no longer worth what it was when they bought it.

> *"The small charity that comes from the heart is better than the great charity that comes from the head."*
> – German proverb

Former President George W. Bush coming off the 18th green at Crooked Stick Golf Course, Indianapolis

Coach Tony Dungy at fundraiser- Super Bowl Champion Colts and Sunday Night Football analyst

Jack and Marge Colescott Golf Tournament-30 year celebration-2019. Left to right, Myrl Nofzinger, Nancy Fitzgerald, Jack Colescott, Terry Munday, Ray Hilbert

Coach Caldwell and wife join us for a fundraiser to raise funds for his charity- Boys and Girls Club

Pacer's Mascot" Boomer" joins us at IWU basketball game

Dr. Ben Carson speaking at the World Changer Induction Ceremony

Grand kids with grandma and grandpa

Munday Family Reunion

Chaparral for seniors- Longview Gardens-Relationship building for planned giving

Family at 50th Wedding Anniversary Celebration

Michael Munday, Marine Corp infantryman veteran of the Afghanistan and Iraq wars

LEFT PHOTO: Family visiting in Washington D.C. We chartered a Lightrider Doubledecker bus and took a 3 day trip with just our family. Good times. This was at the IWO JIMA Memorial

Family at Marion National Cemetary at Michael's gravesite. "Wreath's Across America"

IWU donors, Fred and Leveda Scripture

David Green founder of Hobby Lobby

ALTRUISM OR EGOTISM

I often hear negative comments about donors who have their names placed on buildings. My experience with naming opportunities is that most donors receiving that honor have not asked for the naming opportunity. In the organizations I have worked with, the naming process was initiated by the charity. The donor is simply acting on the organization's request. Is the donor giving because of their love of the institution, the love of the tax advantage, the good feeling that one gets when making a gift, or because of their appreciation for the person making the Ask? There are many reasons why people make major gifts. It is not my responsibility to judge the donor but to make the Ask and attempt to provide every incentive that might be pertinent to the situation. Our goal in fundraising is to receive a favorable response to the Ask. We have found that by naming a building or endowed chair for a donor, others are inspired to become donors themselves. We are always grateful for people who have been successful in their personal finances and are willing to lend their name to a project funded by their gift. Altruism should always prevail.

GIVING AND HAPPINESS

People often wonder if a gift is truly altruistic or is it egotistical. Is there some reward that the donor receives? Aside from all the questions asked, giving has been shown to create happiness in the donor. On the other hand, there are organizations that provide naming opportunities for people other than giving, such as a reward for service or a heroic act of self-service to God or the country. The naming then becomes an act of appreciation and honor. I will let you be the judge if the organization has compromised its charitable mission by not realizing funding for a naming opportunity. However, it is not uncommon for corporations to name buildings for just the advertisement benefit they receive.

DRIVING FORCES

In nonprofits, we define a gift as a voluntary transfer from one party to another without any consideration. But I believe emotion, empathy, or compassion are driving forces in the giving process. Sometimes the "bottom line" is dependent on a donor's state of mind. I recall receiving a call from a lady who was very concerned about having more men involved in teaching at the elementary school level. She was so interested that she wanted to start a scholarship fund that would benefit male elementary teachers. She had some Eagle-Picher stock (roughly $7,000) that she wanted to give to start the fund. Almost immediately, I recalled a conversation with a male elementary student who visited my office to ask for my help in paying off a $7,000 school bill. If he didn't pay the bill it would prevent him from returning for his senior year.

He thought his only answer was to drop out of school and work to save money for paying off his school bill. I shared the story with the lady who wanted to start a scholarship fund and her response was, "Let's pay off his debt now, and start the scholarship in the future." What a joy it was for me to call the student and inform him that he should register for his senior year because his school bill had been paid in full! The story gets even better. One year later I received a call from the donor. She was excited to tell me that by selling the stock, she had not only helped this student, but the company that issued the stock she had given had just declared bankruptcy. If she had held the stock it would have been worthless today. God's guidance in helping us make financial decisions is beyond earthly comparison.

And the "rest of the story?" The young man married shortly after graduation and took a teaching job in elementary education. Afterward, he spent eight years working at an orphanage in Macon, Georgia. And later, the student who "feared he wouldn't make it to his senior year," served as the principal of an International School in China with more than 1,000 students. Was the lady's investment worthwhile? Of course! Did she get as much out of the giving as the student did in the receiving? Absolutely. The lesson is obvious: when God leads, He provides the resources, and then immediately or gradually shows us the way.

ASK AND RECEIVE

Capital campaigns generally focus on the top 10-20% of its donor base but planned giving focuses on everyone. Most people who change their wills do not change the designated gifts in them. Experts are predicting that trillions will be transferred in the next five decades. Yes, that is a T, not an M, in those transfers! Morgan Stanley predicts a third of that money will go to nonprofits (much of it through planned giving). Guess which nonprofits will be receiving the bulk of the transfer? You're right, *those who Ask*! With extended life spans, people are in their prime donor years longer than previous generations. So, with those longer life spans, charities should act soon on the opportunity to capture the support of older donors. Boomers are reaching retirement age, and they want to impact society but are not willing to write a blank check. They want more information regarding how the charity will spend the money. If you are not marketing your planned giving program you are missing the greatest opportunity in the history of fundraising. Too many fundraisers think of security instead of opportunity. We are not following but discovering. Don't fear failure, even a high jumper gets three tries.

Our job is to identify potential donors in our database with whom we will cultivate a relationship to assist them in intergenerational wealth transfers. A study by RBC Wealth Management reported that 30% of Americans surveyed haven't planned their transfer. The Bible talks about "fields that are ripe for harvest." Matching donors with the needs of nonprofits is a ripened field—a Great Handoff. We must be ready with a planned giving program already in place.

WHAT IS A TRILLION

Think about the scope of the transfer: Planned giving will yield $6 trillion to charities over the next 25 years. What does a "trillion" look like? A trillion dollars is a million dollars multiplied by a million. The Calculator Site illustrated it, "If $1 million in $100 dollar bills stacks up to 40 inches (3.3 feet), $1 billion is 40,000 inches high, that's 0.63 miles high! $1 trillion in $100 dollar bills is 40,000,000 inches high, which is 631 miles". Go even farther. A trillion in $1 bills would weigh 10 tons. $1 trillion would fund four years of college, at a $30,000 annual cost, for 8.33 million people. If you spent one dollar every second around the clock, it would take you 31,688 years to spend a trillion dollars. Keep going.

- $1 trillion would buy 41,999,160 new cars
- $1 trillion would fund 20% of U.S. families at $52,029 per year
- $1 trillion would allow spending of $1 million per day for 30,000 years

No one has ever amassed a trillion dollars, but some estimate that Amazon founder and CEO Jeff Bezos, or Microsoft founder, Bill Gates, could be in the running—if their wealth continues to balloon.

SCRIPTURE MANDATE

There is a strong and consistent mandate throughout Scripture for those with wealth to use it to aid those in poverty. The Bible openly gives the method: *giving*. Though giving for its own sake is spiritually and emotionally rewarding, giving with the purpose of empowering others to fulfill their calling is even more rewarding. For example, retirees generally define their success by their giving and not their wealth. Nearly 70% identify generosity as an important source of happiness, and giving creates a higher sense of self-esteem and purpose. Studies show that giving even has a positive influence on levels of depression, blood pressure, and even mortality. It is our association with other individuals who jointly work to benefit a charity that helps us have a greater appreciation for a cause. Plus, it creates a sense of family and community. It was Sir Winston Churchill who said, "We make a living by what we get. We make a life by what we give."

WEALTH AND INCOME

The new laws on the tax policy of 2018 and the volatility of the stock market at the end of 2018 together, may have caused many donors to take another look at their charitable giving. Individuals who once itemized on their tax returns may have lost a charitable deduction with the doubling of the standard deduction. The number of households who deducted in 2016 (more than 45 million) may have dropped to 16-20 million. In most cases, planned giving is from wealth, not income. So, when working with the wealthy we must realize that in many cases they are not giving to their potential ability. They may only be thinking of the income they realize from their wealth when making an annual or planned gift.

Realized income from their wealth is 1-5%, while their total wealth is 20 to 100 times larger than their annual income. As fundraisers, we often consider the amount of the Ask based on income derived from wealth. Giving in death helps the wealthy person give out of their wealth—from 91% of a person's assets while giving out of income is only about 9% of a person's assets.

START SMALL

Claire Axelrad sees a step-up factor in donor giving. "Most 'planned gifts' are major gifts. But not always. Lots of donors give what I call 'token' or 'test' gifts. They give spur of the moment, without a lot of planning or forethought. They're usually new donors who've not yet committed to you in a big way. Or they give because a friend asks them. They're testing the waters. For them to make a more thoughtful or passionate gift in the future, you'll need to engage in some thoughtful, consistent wooing. We normally recommend that good fundraising is spending 75% of the time with the top 10-20% of the donor base, and 25% with those at the bottom of the pyramid

I encourage using the giving philosophies of most colleges—going for larger gifts—but I realize that getting donors started with smaller gifts, at a younger age, can be a major benefit to the charity. Lower level donors develop a sense of ownership in your charity. Over time, they can become recurring gift donors at a higher level, and eventually can be asked to consider a major or planned gift. It is what I call the "Hierarchy of an Ask." Although the process of encouraging smaller gifts is slower in raising funds, it may well be the stabilizing force for charities over the long haul. Younger donors, that is, Millennials, Gen X, Post Millennials, will continue to support our charities for many years, and will eventually make the large gift. Research indicates those individuals who have given 15 or more gifts to a charity will also make a planned gift.

YOU CAN DO IT

I contend that if you have a successful annual fund, you can also have a successful planned giving program. Segment your donor base to determine which of your donors are in the 45-90 year of age segment. The age when most individuals complete a will is between 40-50 years of age. The bulk of planned giving, then, is accomplished through 3 general categories:

1. ***Bequests*** - about 90% of bequests are included in a will.

2. ***Gift Annuities*** - donors receive income for the rest of their life. The percentage they receive is based on their life expectancy (as determined by the Committee on Annuities that meets to assess

rates every 2-3 years). The rate that is set remains constant for the remainder of the annuitants' lifetime. The rate received is usually far better than the rates received from CDs at a bank (the rates are published, and easily assessable). Companies provide a summary for the donor which includes the percentage rate, the tax deduction, and the tax liabilities in the future.

3. ***Gifts of Stock*** - the third most common way a charity receives a planned gift. When a more complex situation arises as part of the planned giving process, the charity can consult with an attorney or financial advisor.

I recommend a more aggressive marketing program for planned giving. For example, I have incorporated it as part of my direct mail program. Each mailing includes a response card that allows the donor an opportunity to notify the charity of their interest in making a planned gift or request a visit from a representative of the charity. Remember, when a donor places your charity in their will, they are putting you alongside those that they love dearly. We should not take that lightly but realize their heart has been endeared to our charity. It is our practice to recognize this planned giving group ("legacy group") each year in a special President's Report.

HELPING THE GENEROUS

The Great Handoff and the economic climate that exists make it more advantageous for donors to make a planned gift. It is important we remind people in our charities that fundraising is not about "selling ice to Eskimos," it is about helping generous people find a way to make a difference in the world. Planned giving should be a part of every charitable organization's development efforts, regardless of the organization's size, mission, age, budget, or giving history. Since it will be helpful in the future, it is important that your organization has a good history and will be viable for 25-50 years in the future.

- Is your organization growing or shrinking?

- How financially stable is your organization?

- Can your organization provide financial reports and information on its overall financial performance?

The *Pareto principle* (also known as the 80–20 rule, the law of the vital few, and the principle of *factor sparsity*), states that for many events, roughly 80% of the effects come from 20% of the causes.

- 80% of sales come from 20% of the salesforce.

- 20% of staff will cause 80% of the problems.

- 20% of the staff will provide 80% of production.

That reminds us to focus on the 20% who matter—on the 20% who will produce 80% of the results.

NO PUSHING

Our job as fundraisers is not to push, pry, force, or coerce anyone, but to have authentic conversations about shared values. Axelrad said, "No one is going to give you an outright major gift unless they have the capacity to do so. Major donors generally have high enough incomes that they can afford to direct some of that income towards charity rather than to themselves, family, or friends. Alternatively, they may have significant assets in an investment portfolio—enough so they can give you some without adversely affecting their own interests. (Bill Gates won't give to you just because he's rich; he must be somehow affiliated with or connected to you and have a demonstrated interest in your cause)."

Again, most donors are giving out of their income rather than from the assets they possess. Unless we offer our constituency a planned giving opportunity, we will continue to receive smaller gifts. In a recent capital campaign, I found that the reason less than 2% of Christians leave planned or deferred gifts to their churches is that, 1) they have not been asked, and 2) they did not know that the church received this type of planned gift.

THE DEVELOPMENT PERSON

It is important to note that having a good annual fund program includes having a planned giving program. It also demonstrates the importance of a good development person. The stability and longevity of staff within the development staff are crucial for relationship development. Normally, when I am interviewing candidates for a position in development or planned giving, I make certain the prospective employee will give a commitment of at least 5 years to the charity before I offer them the position. Research indicates that it takes 7 years to cultivate a planned gift. Fundraisers must have a broad (and continuing) knowledge of giving trends. For example, the graying of our population offers greater opportunities for planned giving. J. Chucks wrote in the *Journal of Aging*, "It is projected that the combined senior and geriatric population will reach 2.1 billion by 2050." [55] In 2018, the state of Florida had the highest percentage of people over the age of 65 in the United States, 19.1%. However, it is estimated that by 2030, 46 US states will have 17% of the age 65 population. It is imperative that all charities become serious about providing their constituency with planned giving opportunities. In the United States. . .

- 69-70% of all gifts come from individuals.

- 15% of all gifts come from foundations.

- 5% of all gifts come from corporations.

But charities will not usually get those gifts unless they *Ask* for it.

TIMES OF CHANGE

Fundraising can be a ministry as well as a profession. As fundraisers, we can be of great help to family survivors. For many years I have been an advocate of family members leaving a "Memo to The Family." In the case of males writing the memo, it would include such instructions as…

- Where they usually get the oil in the car changed.

- Where water or electricity can be turned off.

- Where important papers relating to warranties are kept.

- Where property information is stored.

- Where insurance or investment documents are filed.

- Where wills and bequest documents are filed.

- Password information.

- Funeral and burial instructions.

The female written memo might include much of the same information, along with such items as…

- Family birthday and anniversary dates.

- Family history files.

- Household inventory records.

- Medical information.

- Funeral and burial instructions.

- Distribution of memorabilia and antique instructions.

The memo suggestion may be a simple gesture, but it will be seen as a caring interest by the fundraiser who suggests it—and could relieve major problems for a surviving spouse and other family members.

BOARDS ONBOARD

In every charitable organization, a major effort should be made to get the institution or organization board members to remember it with a planned gift. What a selling point for fundraisers as they represent the charity to its constituency! And, most foundations will ask a charity about the level of support by its board, particularly if 100% are giving at some level.

WORK SMARTER

We must work smarter and spend time cultivating individuals for gifts to our charities. As I've mentioned, often charitable organizations do not receive advance notice that they are included in a bequest. That may be because individuals are reluctant to talk about death and money or because charities have not done an adequate job of informing donors as to the importance of a planned gift.

I recall one occasion when I had delivered to a man named Lloyd a proposal for a music scholarship in the amount of $100,000. I felt he had every intention of establishing a music scholarship, but I had no paperwork or signed agreements regarding the scholarship to music students. After Lloyd died, I received notification from his attorney that IWU would be receiving a scholarship for $100,000. Either he had filed it with his important documents or had simply failed to notify us. About a month later, we received a check for $100,000 from his estate. It would have been so nice to have properly thanked Lloyd for his wonderful gift.

MAKE IT PERSONAL

Personal solicitation is still the best method for securing a gift. I realize the amount of time necessary to make personal visits and make an Ask. But if we wait until everything is perfect before asking, we will probably never make them. Churches will solicit all members on a "Special Offering Sunday" with the intention of getting everyone to participate. It has been my experience that these larger group solicitations will yield proportionally smaller gifts. For that reason, it is important to make personal calls on larger donors before offering everyone an opportunity to give. We call this process a "lead gift phase."

- Many donors in your annual fund program have the potential to become a planned giving prospect.

- 95% of planned gifts are in the form of bequests and annuities and they are the easiest vehicles to help your donors understand.

- Many consider a planned gift because they consider their estate to be a modest size and do not feel they have the resources to make a legacy gift.

- Raising planned gifts can cost 3 to 5 cents per dollar raised.

Again, we have a few people giving a lot and many giving nothing or far too little. The call should be for all people to give if we are going to impact our society's needs. Andrew Murray said, "The world asks, 'What does a man own?' Christ asks, 'How does he use it?'"

Does planned giving make a difference? It did for a couple on the set of IWU's annual "Telesale." I was the emcee for the annual fundraising auction on the University's TV channel. When the phones stopped ringing, I would use the lull as an opportunity to use my unused (and unrecognized) acting talent. The outlandish was my specialty. On one occasion I was wearing a wig and acting out a hair salon scene to advertise the salon. Afterward, a couple from the audience approached me and asked if they could meet me for breakfast. Not knowing whether the invitation was to support my acting career or critique it, I took a chance. It was neither, just the beginning of a wonderful relationship.

When I was invited to their home, I was shocked to see its conditions—no carpeting, sheets and newspaper for window covering, and insulation hanging from the ceiling because of a roof leak. They had indicated they were interested in supporting IWU, but looking around, I thought I might be lucky to see a $1,000 (lifetime) gift. The unmarried couple, Fred and Leveda, slept on a couch in the living room.

Within two months, I suggested to the couple of 40 years that they could save money on their estate taxes if they married. Ross Hoffman stood up with them when they were married before the justice of the peace. Leveda was thrilled at the marriage, but when I suggested that Fred should buy her a dozen roses, he was too frugal to comply. Approximately three months later, my office was astonished to receive a $3.2 million check from them!

Shortly after, Leveda called in tears, saying that during Fred's pre-op for hernia surgery, they discovered he had lung cancer. I rushed to the hospital where Fred would spend the next two months in chemotherapy. Since it was the Christmas season, my staff put together 21 small gifts and a Christmas tree for his room. Each day he would open a gift, and since the first package included a New Testament and a camera, we took pictures of the daily gift opening. I told Fred that I would visit him every day at 7:30 a.m., which I did—even on the weekends. On one Sunday, I told him I was going to pray for his salvation, and that if he wanted, he could pray along with me. At the end of sharing the sinner's prayer, Fred got out of his hospital bed, gave me a big hug, and acknowledged that he had accepted Christ into his life.

Later that week, my staff and I joined a local pastor in baptizing Fred. Leveda had heard what I said to her husband and wanted to accept Christ and be baptized as well. Following Fred's death, she attended church with me and was later admitted to Colonial Oaks nursing home. On her bed was an Indianapolis Colts blanket I gave her—and it remained there till her death. The rest of Fred and Leveda's estate totaled $6 million, and their name is on a campus dorm to honor their memory. I praise God for Fred and Leveda. And I praise God for a planned giving program that transferred their wealth directly into the lives of IWU students.

"Family is more important than this business."
– David Green

CHAPTER 7

Call to Action:
The Immediate and The Eternal

A sign on the digital billboard of a local bank said, "Here Today, Here Tomorrow." It certainly is a catchy phrase, but it is a promise it cannot keep. In fact, it can't even promise it will be there for the rest of the day. Jesus said, "We must quickly carry out the tasks assigned us by the one who sent us. The night is coming, and then no one can work" (John 9:4 NLT). Every Christian organization has an immediate and eternal mission. It does what it is called to do in the immediate, believing it is making an eternal impact.

THE IMMEDIATE

I believe God created life and gave His creation the resources to live it. He also gave His creation a responsibility to make choices that will affect each stage of that life. Immediate choices, including financial, have eternal consequences. No, you "can't take it with you," but you can plan what happens to it before you leave. Every person and every organization has an "immediate" to consider when it comes to the intergenerational transfer of wealth.

First, the great transfer is more reality than expectancy. It is happening now. Millions of dollars are being passed along—clumsily or carefully. Some will gain from it and others will be the losers. The "gainers" will be those who prepare for the transfer and act upon it. It is the same for every organization: immediate decisions, eternal consequences. In the last decade, the number of non-profits has increased by 23.4% while individual giving has increased by only 3.4%. Smith and Clurman wrote, "New market trends wrought by generational differences are causing business upheavals, bringing new categories into being at warp speed, and causing old ones to shrink or disappear."[56]

Second, the transfer of wealth will come largely from Baby Boomers and the Silent Generation—which makes it important to charities and fundraisers to work across generational lines to realize giving potential. Between 1946 and 1964, 77 million babies were born in the US. Today, those Boomers are 28% of the population who will be a vital part of *The Great Handoff.* The Silent Generation, which currently controls about $11 trillion of US assets will share their current assets through estate plans and bequests to younger generations in the next 10-15 years. And overall net wealth will grow by about $50 trillion during the next 15 years. In her book, *Donor-Centered Leadership,* Penelope Burk said, "We're right in the midst of the perfect age demographic for Baby Boomers' putting planned gifts in their wills. This is right now, and we're about to miss it." 2019 figures estimate that Boomer households control 54% of total US households' net worth while Millennials control only 4% household net worth. Boomers spend over $548 billion annually, about $300 billion more than Gen X. Trillions (with a T) will change hands. And Boomers will remain a primary target as prospective donors for the next two decades. After 2030, the financial assets of Boomers will begin to decline because of higher death rates. The unknown factor: 1) Will the transfer actually take place, or will

Boomers spend it all on lavish living—and trying to prolong life? And, 2) Will the transfer go to children or to charity?

The *Chronicle of Philanthropy* found that wealthier Americans gave less of their income to a charity during the Recession. But from 2015 through 2030, US household assets are expected to increase from $87 trillion to $140 trillion. Of this amount, $64 trillion will be considered investable financial assets. An uptick is already on the monitor. Giving to charity has increased in total dollars given. During 2018, more than $400 billion was given to charity—and nearly 75-80% of that giving came from individuals and families.

What to do in a "roller-coaster economy?" When Madison Avenue experiences downturns, it steps up marketing and sales. Charities will need to do the same thing through planned giving. They will need to:

- Add planned giving programs.
- Hire fundraising professionals.
- Collect donor data.
- Produce marketing materials and media.
- Expand their online presence.

Charities that fail to make planned giving and major gifts a priority upfront will end up needing them as a last resort. I see areas of real concern. *One,* not-for-profits seem to be focusing primarily on "megagifts" received from the wealthy. For example, March of Dimes is concentrating on larger donors and has quit soliciting donors of $15 or less. *Two,* some charities seem to fear the allocating of funds to acquire lower or mid-level donors. Wealthier donors are highly important to a charity's future, but not at the expense of gaining lower and mid-level donors—and the potential for added gifts and future giving. Donors who give million-dollar gifts have usually given 15-20 annual gifts *prior* to making the major gift. Never minimalize the smaller donations. Lately, I've heard of several charities that have abandoned fundraising events because they were "too labor-intensive." I know from experience how much work goes into managing fundraising events—and the long hours it takes to bring them to fruition.

> *"The best thing to do with the best things in life is to give them away."*
> – Dorothy Day

But I've found that an added value of an event goes beyond monies raised, to forming relationships with event volunteers. I've watched as they've caught the charity's vision while they assisted with an event. And I've noticed that many of those volunteers are now on the charity's donor list. We must *anticipate* that over time, volunteers will likely become major gift donors or planned giving prospects. It continues to be important to have a *giving pyramid* with a large base of donors. Instead, the pyramid base has become more restricted and becomes more like the lead of a pencil—gradually being reduced with use. As we go to the same top donors regularly, their numbers continue to dwindle—perhaps from "donor fatigue."

Three, minority groups must have greater participation in the inheritance scene. An analysis found that 23% of white Americans had already received an inheritance while only 11% of black Americans were recipients—and only 4% of recipients were Hispanics. We know that groups with lower incomes usually have fewer assets to transfer as an inheritance. Despite large gains in income, minorities have not accumulated as many assets to pass on as bequests. During the last decade, the median income among African Americans rose 34%, while their median inheritance rose only 12%. More than 50% of all black households with a member 70 years or older have no financial assets and nothing to bequeath.

For Hispanics, the median income is $30,000. Interestingly, one of the reasons many have failed to accumulate more in savings may be that nearly half of the wage earners send money to support their families in their country of origin. Sending money as they earn it, results in a lack of accumulated funds for their retirement. Race and ethnicity also factor into inheritance size as it relates to income. Bequests from Latinos and Asians averaged $94,000 and $76,100 respectively, compared to $55,100 for whites and $44,000 for blacks. While the net worth of white American families has risen by 40% over the last decade, African American and Hispanic families have seen their net worth rise only by 16%.

Disparities are also seen in generational lifestyles.

- Baby Boomers who finished college had well-paying jobs and saved enough funds for a down payment on a home after 3 years, while Millennials will need to save funds for 19 years to afford a home deposit.

- Only 1/3 of Millennials own their own homes compared to 2/3 of Baby Boomers at the same age.

- Millennials spend 25% of their income on housing, while Baby Boomers spend 6%.

- According to Wells Fargo studies, only 40% feel good about their savings toward retirement. Ramit Sathe popularized the concept of "conscious spending" in his book, *I Will Teach You to be Rich*. He emphasizes the need to decide where to direct your money rather than spend your money impulsively.

- Boomers may "spend down" their wealth rather than continue to accumulate—but they may also live longer.

Between 2031 and 2045, 10% of the total wealth in the US will change hands every 5 years. This, and the generational differences in expectations, will require major changes. As mentioned, the average net worth of Silent Generation retirees 75 years and older is $264,750. Most locked into lower home mortgage rates in the '60s, resulting in less debt. In contrast, the average net worth of Millennials is $100,800., with an average debt of $42,000. So intergenerational wealth transfer can be a great benefit to younger generations.

College loan debt will remain a primary financial concern among Millennials and Post-Millennials. Jenna Spinelle wrote in *Credit Sesame*, "According to the New York Federal Reserve, total student loan debt in the US currently stands at $1.26 trillion spread among more than 43 million borrowers." She said that among the company's nearly 500 million members ages 18-34, they owe a collective $10.5 billion in student loans.[57] Wealth transfer may be a break in the lingering student loan clouds. Boomers will gift some of their assets to children and grandchildren while they are still alive, to enjoy their influence on kids and grandkids. Next Gens can use those gifts to pay off high-interest debt. And that wise use of monies could have a positive, continual effect. When I counsel families, I always advise them to set aside six months' worth of savings for living expenses. If they have a sudden loss of income, the results could be devastating. I also counsel families who receive an inheritance to put it into a separate bank account. If blended in with other funds, inheritance monies will be too easy to spend. Giving USA gave us these "Immediate" imperatives for charities and fundraisers:

1. Build a more compelling case for giving. There are more than one million non-profit organizations vying for those dollars.

2. Improve online and social media communications with donors.

3. Gain a broader audience by partnering with other organizations.

4. Improve efforts in getting small annual gifts from constituents.

5. Shift priorities from fundraising to solving problems specific to the community.[58]

When *Forbes* brought 150 billionaires together to talk about ways to solve the world's problems, the following key themes emerged: 1. They want to see results of their philanthropy during their lifetime, and are less interested in leaving a legacy; 2. They are willing to partner with others to ensure greater effectiveness; 3. They are willing to risk failure in order to be more effective over time; 4. They plan to give their money away during a short time frame of 10 years. What do these key findings mean to charities who want to make an effective Ask of the wealthy? Charities must act quickly. They need to immediately determine the hot button concerns of potential donors. And they need to study the issues that have prompted donor giving in the past—and then ask, "Does our mission align or coincide with their interests?"

THE ETERNAL

"Right now, counts forever," author and Presbyterian minister, R. C. Sproul, once wrote. He's right. The rivers of life have a continual flow and as they do, their ripples and waves leave marks on their shoreline. In my book, *It's Not About the Money*, I said that my rewards for decades of fundraising for various institutions and charities have been more than monetary. I have had the opportunity to meet thousands of people who have shaped my understanding of money, giving, and God's work in my life.

So, who will shape the understanding of the next generations? That question has been answered in my own home where my wife Linda and

I have committed our parental and grandparent lives to teach our family about the things that matter most.

We haven't lived sheltered lives on some remote island; we have lived as believers in Christ on the main streets of small or larger towns or cities. And we have lived among those who have either done life their way or God's way. I believe that every person who is responsible for either raising or man-

> *"There can be no Christianity where there is no charity"*
> – Charles Caleb Colton

aging monies in the name of the Lord has an obligation to teach others about money management. I have utilized "off the clock" time to do just that. I'm using my professional "work skills" to influence and disciple others to apply biblical principles in their "life skills."

What matters most? For many, the answer is obviously entertainment. The Bureau of Labor Statistics said that in 2017, US home entertainment average spending was at nearly $10 billion. Those figures included expenditures for DVD sales, electronics, on-demand streaming subscriptions, and others. It wouldn't be a stretch to say that entertainment is teaching our generation and the next a worldview that is 360-degrees off a biblical view. That troubles me as a fundraiser and troubles me as a father and grandfather.

It is understood that a person's worldview is developed between the ages of 18 months and 13 years. According to the research of religious pollster George Barna, the worldview young people have at 13 years old is the worldview they will die with. Parenting is one of the most important factors in shaping the values of their children—and Millennials are entering their prime childbearing years. Education begins in the home. Nancy Fitzgerald, a friend of many years, has spent most of her life trying to help young people develop a Christian worldview. She said that one's worldview begins to be formed earlier, at *2 years*, and continues through age 13. Our churches and pastors must act quickly if they are going to teach parents the value of a Christian worldview. They must address issues such as marriage definition, sexuality and alternative lifestyles, human rights—including the rights of the unborn—and money management from a biblical position, otherwise, the culture will mold their child's worldview from its own position.

I'm not only concerned about *what* shapes the generations that follow, I am also concerned about *who* is shaping it. For example, Millennials have generally received their religious training from their college rather than their church. A study by Neil Gross and Solon Simmons found that approximately 25% of college professors are professing atheists or agnostics while the general population is 5-7% atheist or agnostic. And not only did 51% of those professors describe the Bible as "an ancient book of fables, legends, history and moral precepts," 75% believe religion does not belong in our educational systems. Many colleges teach students that life is about asking questions, not about believing dogmatic answers. So, what WILL shape the thinking and behavior of a generation that lacks the absolutes of the Bible? Perhaps the answer is already being revealed through several philosophies that exist—and are gaining greater acceptance.

Humanism is the first philosophy of concern. The dictionary describes it as a "system of values and beliefs based on the idea that people are basically good and that problems can be solved using reason instead of religion." In other words, thought without religious influence. My concern about the re-emergence of this 14th-century philosophy is that it sees itself as its own Source. Instead of believing that "Every good and perfect gift is from above, *coming down* from the Father of the heavenly lights" (James 1:17, emphasis mine), humanism believes that "good" and "perfect" come *from within*—from a person's self-efforts. Put in context, life decisions (including financial), have no guide but the wisdom and whims of self. The result is a spirit of ingratitude and indulgence without guardrails. George Barna wrote, "The Bible no longer holds the revered place in society that it once had. Most households (91%) still own one or more copies of the Bible, but barely one-third of all adults believe that it is totally accurate in all of the principles it teaches." [59]

I have observed that since prayer and the Bible have been taken out of the classroom, they are increasingly missing from the lifestyles of individuals and families. Interestingly, they are missing from those very people who will eventually realize the poverty of self-effort and will desperately seek wisdom beyond themselves. Author and *TIME* magazine contributor, Mary Eberstadt, asserts, "The fortunes of religion rise or fall with the state of the family."

Secularism is the second philosophy of concern. Merriam-Webster defines it as "indifference to or rejection or exclusion of religion and religious considerations." In other words, culture without religious influence. But faithless cultures end in faithless ruins. Think Roman Empire or the Third Reich. Jesus lived in such a culture, calling it an "unbelieving generation" (Mark 9:19), and sought to teach it about the things that matter more than the immediate. Amenable to no one, the secularist feeds on his or her own "gusto." Secularism grabs all it can in any way it can—without the wisdom of God—and *cans* what it gets—without real concern for the needs of others. Stuff is king. "Get it while it's "in" and on sale—and trade up when it needs replacement!" It is an Amazon-think culture, only a mouse-click and a 24-hour delivery removed from perceived happiness.

Universalism is another philosophy of concern. It is a user-friendly belief that is all-inclusive. In other words, religion without righteousness.

Scripturally, it is the "form of godliness" without spiritual power. The church itself has become vulnerable to this deceptive belief that equates goodness and good works with salvation. Universalism serves its perceived "user-friendly God," who will send everyone to heaven and no one to hell. But Jesus said there is a distinctive, "I am the way and the truth and the life. *No one* comes to the Father *except through* me" (John 14:6, emphasis mine). Universalism suggests there are alternate routes, (and alternate gods instead of Jehovah God). Consequently, its unwitting adherents believe that the Bible is irrelevant for modern times—including as counsel for modern finances.

> *"Faith is to believe what you do not see; the reward of this faith is to see what you believe."*
> – St. Augustine

Where do I stand? I stand with the biblical giant, Joshua, who said: "As for me and my house, we will serve the Lord" (Joshua 24:15). I wholeheartedly believe that I cannot save myself from who I am or from what I have done. I need a savior-deliverer, someone who will break the chains of a ME that was born in sin and give me hope beyond my efforts. And years ago, I found that hope through personal faith in the Lord Jesus Christ. I acknowledged my sin, put my trust in the One who paid the price of my rebellion against God with His own life. He put His Spirit within me to guide me in all my decisions—finances included. I believe that He is not *A* hope, He is *THE* hope, the only religious leader whose validity is proven by an empty grave following His death.

Christianity is arguably one of the most generous of all religions. Its humanitarian efforts track to Old Testament times and its efforts to aid the needy. Its modern efforts are carried out by Christian nonprofits who are meeting needs around the clock, around the world. Philanthropy means "love of humanity." It is more than the rich trying to avoid taxes and more than an attempt to improve society. It is more than money and more than dressing for the wealthy. It should not just be focused on the materialism that is inadvertently being passed to the next generation. We should be passing on a biblical Legacy that values a lifestyle that includes living within a practical budget, avoiding debt by avoiding unnecessary expenditure, and the practice of generous giving to others. Jim Caraway, a highly successful oil businessman, said, "Making a lot of money and spending it on yourself is not a lot of fun." He concluded, "What is a lot of fun is to live modestly so that you can

> *"The purpose of life is not to be happy. It is to be useful, to be honorable, to be compassionate."*
> – Ralph Waldo Emerson

give to the common good. That's where happiness really lies." I agree. The Great Handoff must be more than just trading dollars and trust funds and properties and collectibles, any of which can be lost in an instant. Rather, it must be more about treasures of the heart. Jesus said, "Do not store up for yourselves treasures on earth, where moth and rust destroy, and where thieves break in and steal. But store up for yourselves treasures in heaven, where moth and rust do not destroy, and where thieves do not break in and steal. For where your treasure is, there your heart will be also" (Matthew 13:19-20).

Many parents divide their estate equally between their children without regard to their spiritual commitment, financial need, or responsibility. A friend told me the story of his mother and her only brother. Raised in the home of her evangelist father and a mother who was also a pastor, his mother chose to follow Christ at an early age and after college, began a 45-year traveling music ministry with her husband. They had a meager income, living off small "love offerings" from churches where they ministered. But thanks to frugal spending and careful money management, they retired debt-free—in a home they paid for with their *savings*. Her brother decided not to follow Christ. After college and tours in the Navy, he married and became an executive with a large company. His lifestyle was totally opposite from his sister's—with harmful habits and lavish spending that led to bankruptcy and the loss of his oft-mortgaged home. His large salary bought him everything but happiness. So, what if we divide an estate equally, and one uses it for the advancement of the Kingdom while the second squanders it with financial irresponsibility and selfish living? Are we indiscriminately passing it to the next generation without considering the impact of Kingdom work? I admit those are highly sensitive questions that call for wise and careful answers.

So, after 30 years of fundraising, consulting, and serving in Christian higher education, permit me to share the framework of a plan that I believe would reverse harmful trends and make a difference both for the immediate time and for eternity.

1. Teach a balanced view of money and wealth. *Wall Street Journal* columnist, Jason Zweg, notes "Doing and being are better than having." Most of our work as fundraisers or administrators is about financial gain— coming out ahead instead of falling behind. And rightfully so. Our objective is to help stakeholders reach their financial objectives, goal by goal. Yet, we can't lose sight of the fact that financial gain is not an end in itself; it is only a means. My lifetime of aiding Christian charities with fundraising needs that will help them for years to come has given me great personal satisfaction. At the same time, I have never lost sight of values that aren't listed on financial statements. My greatest work is measured by eternal gain. And my greatest hope is that none of my clients will think that "gaining the whole world" is worth "forfeiting their own soul." As I've said before, if we are asking for a Christian cause, we'd better be asking in order to advance the kingdom of God and not our own position. So, even as we solicit funding, we must show donors how the wealth they share will bring even greater value to the lives of those who benefit from a charity's mission—as well as benefiting themselves.

2. Practice good money management. We know that "charity begins at home," but so does planning and savings and investing. We wouldn't trust a guide who has never been to the spot they propose to help us find. Personally, I wouldn't want to be left hanging because someone didn't know the ropes. Neither would your clients or donors. Most every American knows how to spend money, but many don't know how to manage it. Often, 2nd and 3rd generations of wealth become lazy and complacent with their money and burn through it in 10 or so years. They think mom and dad and grandparents will keep the money flowing. I know of some very wealthy people who transferred hundreds of millions of dollars as an inheritance to children who later filed for bankruptcy. It is important that parents who were successful in acquiring money teach their children how to use money to replicate itself. We all want to pass along monetary gifts to our children. However, it is extremely important that what we give doesn't harm them more than help them.

Plan your estate transfer. Clients and donors must know that you have a path to their future, but first, you must carve out your own. Guiding others through the steps of estate planning is easier when you've been through the same steps yourself.

- Inventory your resources (cash, property, collectibles).
- Identify your beneficiaries (spouse, children, grandchildren, charities).
- Decide your distribution percentages (who gets what).
- Execute a will (put it in writing).

What factors will influence the decisions of your heirs? Values, experiences, societal and cultural norms? Will they spend it on themselves or will they fail to decide and let the government choose? The importance of your own planning and the wisdom you have attempted to instill in their lives could be of great help in their making good financial decisions.

Practice honesty and openness. "Fake" is the new watchword for everything from the morning news to late evening infomercials on TV. Honesty has been the best policy since that supposed first usage of the phrase in America's first English settlement at Jamestown, Virginia. Obviously, some have lost the "honesty-is-the-best-policy" in translation. Ponzi schemes have given way to online scams that have bilked billions from people who have invested their life savings in a "too good to be true" pitch.

Budget with frugality. Which do you prefer, being rich or being happy? Wealth does not always lead to happiness. Wealth doesn't guarantee fulfillment. How do we become content with what we have? That is a question every charity, fundraiser, client, or donor must decide. I know of charities that have closed their doors because they spent too much time gazing through the window of opportunity—then overreaching and overbuilding in light of their underfunding. These steps backward have thrown perfect missions off course. The same principles apply at street level. We live in a consumer-oriented culture where materialism thrives, which makes it hard to learn to be content. We need to break the habit of satisfying our discontent with acquisitions. We need to refuse a comparison of the *Who* and *What* of others.

After practicing a frugal lifestyle for 50-plus years, it is a habit that I never intend to break. I am more comfortable in carefully preparing for retirement than carelessly spending on the present. I've never missed the trinkets and toys that I could have purchased along the way. I have never felt less competent or deprived wearing a Stafford suit purchased at Sears or one from an after Christmas sale at Dillards. I have been known to drive a used car or truck that holds a salvage title. When I purchase an appliance for my home, I have a habit of looking at the "scratch and dent" section before making the purchase. By using discretion in my spending, I can pay my tithe and still have money to give others—and help my children and grandchildren. Former Notre Dame University public relations director, James W. Frick, said, "Don't tell me where your priorities are. Show me where you spend your money and I'll tell you what they are."

Buy now, pay later is a time bomb philosophy—with a shorter fuse than imagined. Impulsive purchases and consumer debt are not acceptable habits for frugal living. They use future income to pay for current expenditures. (I have seen credit cards that charge above 20% interest!) Delayed material gratification is the best practice.

- The person with no consumer debt has delayed gratification.
- The ability to invest money now for retirement is delayed gratification.

Financial advisors recommend saving 10% of your lifetime earnings for retirement. But of the 10,000 Baby Boomers heading into retirement per day, 42% of them have not *started* saving for retirement. Insured Retired Institute reports that 24% of Baby Boomers have no retirement; therefore, approximately 50% will be living off Social Security benefits (40% of which they are normally expected to generate from their retirement income). And Social Security benefits paid to 84% of retirees are at an average of $1,317 per month (which is less than their average wage). Baby Boomers were affected by the 2008-2009 stock market decline. The following seven years of low-interest rates resulted in slower growth in savings accounts.

Catch a new vision. Wealthy people know how to *make* money while rich people only *have* money. Sometimes people who are considered rich are living or drowning in debt. The difference is in their vision—or lack thereof. One financial planning company advertises that it will assist clients in directing their wealth, "creating clarity about who you are and what you care about." That is spot on for visionary money management. One of baseball great Yogi Berra's famous saying has more truth than humor, "The future ain't what it used to be." He's right. The future has changed along with the culture. People or charities that operate with a 20th-century vision will stumble in a 21st -century economy.

3. Proactively teach the next generations how to handle money. Our family members must know at the earliest in life, how to accrue, spend, save, and invest money. Post-Korean War generations of Americans have become "see-it, buy-it consumers." Madison Avenue makes the call and consumers answer—usually on their pay per month cellphone service. Whether the "call" is about the latest Apple Watch, Samsung cellphone, Starbucks latte, or Tommy Hilfiger jacket, modern consumers have their *Visa* card in hand—and are willing to max it out for the sake of crowd approval. Age, race, and gender influence wealth, but delaying gratification beat out many of the more traditional signals. Temple University found that a tendency to indulge in instant gratification can relate to the abuse of addictive substances, and addictive behavior.

Of course, the see-it, buy-it culture isn't new, and it could be the result of "deprived" parents who want to ensure that their kids have what they never had. They didn't consider the fallout of raising next generation kids who lack drive, creativity, or passion. And little did they think that inheritance in the hands of the irresponsible would result in a plague of irresponsibility. In his book, *Inherited Wealth,* author John Levy said that some kids feel guilty for their inheritance; they fail to face life challenges, and the fear of losing the wealth has been passed along to them. The consequences are a call to action. We must be people who teach our children and grandchildren the "facts of money." From penny jar banks to starter checking accounts, to lemonade sales, our curriculum must be the stuff of Main Street before we get to Wall Street.

I learned money management from parents who lived on a farm, milked cows by hand, and sold product to a local cheese factory. I watched them squeeze money from a dollar at home and in their small construction business. Dad had a sixth-grade education and Mom had a high school diploma, but the education they gave me about handling money has served me like a Harvard Business school degree. As a former history teacher, I am not sure that we taught the value of delayed gratification as part of our economics or history courses. But as a fundraiser, I want to be sure to teach people the wise use of their hard-earned dollars.

4. Promote planned giving. Any charity that says it can't afford a planned giving program, may eventually put one in place out of desperation to save their programs or properties from extinction. Trillions of dollars in intergenerational wealth will be waiting the right Ask to share the mission of the charity that does the asking. Restaurants can have 5-star food, staff, or advertising, but they'll never get a return customer until that first customer recommends it to someone who is hungry. Fundraisers, in particular, must be *customers* before they can be advertisers or staff members who prepare "meals." Every high traffic website will likely have a "Learn More" button. With just a mouse click, information about a subject, program, or product will pop up. Charities and fundraisers must be "Learn More" people, willing to invest time in learning how to draw donors in—and keep them until their interest results in action. I'll never forget that call from a lady who was a benefactor of a million-dollar life insurance policy—and didn't know how to invest it. I immediately became her "Learn More" source (and the referral person for a Christian higher education institution)!

5. Use wealth for its greater good. The spending that is under our management must be used in a purposeful and redemptive way. Charity balance sheets should track receivables and payables to make sure the payables reflect generosity to the needs of others while practicing conservative administrative costs. Riches in the world aligns itself with a self-indulgent heart while the wealthy in the Scriptures see themselves as stewards of God's gifts and manage them to glorify Him. Baby Boomers are often self-described workaholics, but they must not think of themselves as better than others because of their material gain. One's hope must not be in a good job or bank account. Why? Proverbs 23:5 says, those things can "sprout wings and fly off to the sky like an eagle."

Our responsibility to donors does not stop at collecting checks. We are also responsible to teach them how to deepen their faith through giving. To use wealth for its greater good. With the deterioration of values in America, I am very concerned that we pass on to our families more than our material possessions. We must give them an example of walking in a way that exemplifies God-honoring values.

I believe that God has a reason for entrusting these trillions of dollars to us. And maybe one of those reasons is His desire to see how we will use them to expedite the fulfillment of the Great Commission. Business leader, Fred Smith, said that after we have become successful, we must say, "God has given me something to develop, so it is my responsibility to take that and do as much as I can with it."

"The thing we fear most is having lived our lives pleasantly,
but to have made no measurable difference whatsoever."
– Lloyd John Ogilvie

CHAPTER 8

Systems and Strategy

United Airlines flight 232 was heading to Chicago when engine failure in the tail of the DC-10 severed hydraulic lines. Trying to land at a nearby airport, the plane crashed and cartwheeled off the runway, killing 110 souls on board. The crash led the FAA to require redundant safety systems in all future aircraft.[60] In the airline industry, systems and strategy combine to make for a successful flight and smooth landing. But when they are not operational or in synch, they can lead to a disaster.

Systems and strategy are also important in fundraising—and can result in either a successful flight or an emergency landing. Sadly, some organizations are not utilizing them or using those that are obsolete—like trying to draw business travelers to a flight on a biplane. Granted, both the sleek airplane and the cumbersome biplane are using the same aeronautical principles, but one is reaching its destination easier and safer. In this chapter, we'll unwrap what I said were the systems easiest to ask for, and the least complicated to administer, in a planned giving program:

147

- Wills (Bequests)

- Annuities

- Charitable Remainder Trusts

- Appreciated Stock

They are not intended to replace standard fundraising methods, rather, they are the overall focus of a planned giving emphasis to raise monies for the ***annual fund*** (monies raised to help nonprofits cover operational expenses—and targeted campaigns for specific projects). Beyond that, they are giving instruments that donors and nonprofits use to link causes and interests and resources to better society. Jerold Panas, co-founder and chairman of the Institute for Charitable Giving, which specializes in training and coaching professionals in the field, said, "People give to your organization to create change. No one gives to maintain the status quo. Men and women don't want to give money away. They want to give to bold and dazzling programs that are transformative." [61]

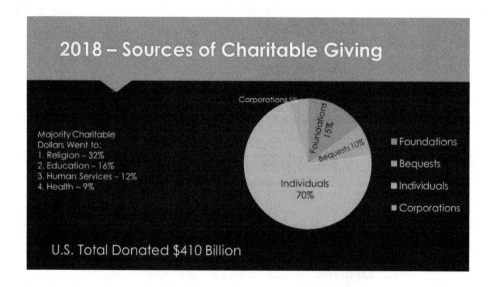

2018 – Sources of Charitable Giving

Majority Charitable
Dollars Went to:
1. Religion – 32%
2. Education – 16%
3. Human Services – 12%
4. Health – 9%

Corporations 5%
Foundations 15%
Bequests 10%
Individuals 70%

- Foundations
- Bequests
- Individuals
- Corporations

U.S. Total Donated $410 Billion

LEGACY GIVING

Given the magnitude and importance of intergenerational wealth transfers, we must encourage donors to consider planned gifts—not only to minimize taxes but to maximize benefits for their heirs and nonprofits of their choice. In other words, to leave a legacy. Most donors are aware of the challenges of distributing wealth to children or spouses in a way that makes their lives better, not worse. planned giving gives them a proven way to distribute wealth in a correct, practical, and equitable way. Benjamin Franklin said, "Well done is better than well said." In other words, life rewards action. We need to get a plan and then work our plan.

Estate attorneys and financial advisors should receive much credit for the origin of planned gifts. For that reason, I included local attorneys and financial advisors from Edward Jones, etc. to information sessions of the University. They were also placed on committees and advisory boards to increase their knowledge of the University and to gain from their knowledge and experience. Charitable organizations have received planned gifts without a definite and proactive, planned giving program. However, that may lead to a false sense of security and may mean that those organizations without a plan may end up with a smaller piece of The Great Handoff. Those who plan and work the planned giving spectrum will benefit from their efforts. I recommend that organizations with limited resources consider making the annual fund and planned giving work together. Both have similar component parts: identifying, cultivating, and asking. Remember, a donor's history of giving is one of the most important variables for legacy prospects. You don't need an attorney on staff, but a relationship with an attorney or alliance with other professionals.

The cost to solicit donations in the US is $1 for every $6 collected, but the results are incalculable. Also, the impact on fundraising staff and volunteers is not shown on summary reports; it is shown in their hearts. So, we might say that the heart of fundraising is the heart. What is its value, and how will it positively impact others? Of course, for Christian non-profits, values are born from a belief in the Word of God as a standard of behavior and its methods always seek eternal results. For example, history has seen the rise and fall of several religious TV personalities who gradually moved from evangelism to entrepreneurship, building massive real estate holdings, and accepting exorbitant salaries in the process. Their core message remained the same, but their "sleight of hand" in using standard fundraising methods for personal gain brought shame to the church and its people. Thankfully God will never go back on His Word and will honor its message, even if it is preached by less than honorable messengers.

PURPOSE-DRIVEN EVENTS

Fundraising events are a time-proven method for raising interest in and supporting your mission. And it must be remembered that every event or activity done in the name of a parent organization is a reflection on the values of that organization. The event or activity may be pure, but its actions and actors may bring more frowns than smiles. I think there are at least four questions that can be used in planning or implementing a fundraising event.

1. What is the bottom-line purpose of this event?

2. What does this event say about the values and character of the organization?

3. How do the plans of the event represent the core purpose of the organization?

4. Will any event activity cause someone to feel important or will it make them feel uncomfortable?

5. Do any activities of the event seem "out of character" for the organization?

Author and social impact leader, Janet Levinger, said, "Fundraising can be scary and hard. But if you focus on values, people will see it as an expression of what we most cherish about our organization." She tells of how it was applied in her membership on a nonprofit's board,

> "I was on the board of an organization that focused on a vulnerable, low-income population. One thing I admired about this organization was that in addition to having vision and mission statements, we had a strong value statement with clear values about telling the truth, taking risks, and treating everyone with respect. Another value was about looking for new and creative ways to address problems. The last was about community and integrity." [62]

5-STAR EVENTS

Fundraising is a science resulting from multiple experiments (events), a science that builds donor relationships as well as funds. I believe there are common principles upon which successful events are built. In hospitality ratings, 5 stars represent excellence. I'm sure you would not expect anything less than a 5-Star rating for your event. Like points in a star, there are 5 preparation points that lead to event Excellence: Purpose, Planning, Personnel, Promotion, and Pursuit.

1. PURPOSE IS THE EVENT'S "WHY?"

An event without a pre-determined purpose will always have undetermined results. Even if it is multifaceted, each facet should connect to the event purpose—and subsequently to the values and image of the parent organization. That purpose could be described in a sentence or two that includes goals and objectives. For example, each year Indiana Wesleyan University would host a Founder's Day Celebration where we would seek to raise $50,000-$150,000 for a specific project needed on campus. We would invite those individuals who had given at the Indiana Tax Credit level ($400). The projects might include the purchase of science equipment for the physics and biology departments or a project that included the athletic department. A video would highlight activities in both departments demonstrating how the new equipment would impact student learning. We would feature 2-3 students who provided testimonials that generally stirred an emotional moment, followed by an opportunity to make gifts or pledges.

2. PLANNING IS THE EVENT'S "WHAT?"

A coordinator could be appointed to chair meetings of an appointed event committee. Its members should be chosen to reflect their interests and skills for the event activities—and reflect their "track record" in following orders, personal initiative, teamwork, and follow-through. Committee activities should include:

- Approving event activities, with brief descriptions, deadlines, and to-do lists.

- Establishing a budget to include projected costs and funding for advertising, materials, housing, meals, transportation, and honoraria.

- Approving event staffing.

3. PERSONNEL IS THE EVENT'S "WHO?"

Events are people-driven—and people-focused. Everyone on the event "support team" should receive a brief job description in advance and a thank-you note afterward. This year IWU celebrated the 30th year of the Jack and Marge Colescott Golf Tournament. The golf outing has raised more than a million dollars for student scholarships for students in Grant County. The tournament has required the assistance of hundreds of volunteers who have given many hours in making the tournament a success. These volunteers have driven golf carts, delivered snacks to participants, made signs and posters, registered guests, and took photographs of the participants. Many of these same volunteers and participants have become planned giving prospects.

4. PROMOTION IS THE EVENT'S "WHEN?" AND "WHERE?"

Site reservation and preparation are important to the success of an event. Schedulers and property managers should not be the last to know. Check the calendar and then make sure the event is on it—with the event coordinator's contact information. Community calendars should also be considered so conflicting events don't jeopardize your event's attendance. And then, PROMOTE, PROMOTE, PROMOTE! The "best deal in town" is worthless unless potential customers are asking, "What's the deal, and where can I get it?" Details rule! There are at least 9 questions that should be answered in promotion media:

1. What is the event?
2. Who is sponsoring it?
3. How will it benefit me?
4. Where will it be held?
5. When will it be held?
6. What is the starting time?

7. How much does it cost?

8. How do I become involved?

9. Who do I contact?

5. PURSUIT IS THE EVENT'S "HOW?"

When all is said and done, what will be said when it is done? A successful event isn't finished when the lights are turned off. The "How" of an event is measured in

- "How did we do in accomplishing its purpose?"

- "What are the long-term results?"

- "How will the results be turned into resources?"

- "What's next?"

But events aren't just about performance; they are also about the pursuit. For instance, your event registration list is a potential donor list that includes people who must be pursued—even beyond their immediate gift or pledge. Remember, your "purpose" is to gain both interest *and* investment. Each year we would ask best-selling author, Dr. John C. Maxwell, to give us a day of his time that we could turn into scholarship money. He graciously consented and for several years we were able to raise $119,000-$130,000 to support the cause. We would schedule John for a speaking engagement on leadership in Indianapolis in the morning and then transport him by helicopter to either Cincinnati, Fort Wayne, or Louisville. The results were fantastic as 2,500-3,000 people were exposed to IWU and its mission.

At the intermission, we would pass out door prizes to guests who dropped their business cards into a box for a drawing. Those business cards became the registration invitees for the next year's seminar. It also gave me an opportunity to visit many CEOs and HR directors during the next year as we sought to expand our adult student enrollment base.

MAJOR GIFTS

Successful events have included dinners, auctions, marathons, telethons, concerts, tours, et al. They join other top-tier fundraising methods, such as direct mail, social media, product sales, credit card affiliations, memorials, and building or chair naming to supplement a planned giving program. Every gift is important, but if your organization is to have a sustainable income, it must develop a "major gift" initiative.

Major gifts take 9-12 months to cultivate, but their importance is in raising larger amounts of money at a much lower cost to the organization. Major gift campaigns and capital campaigns can pay major dividends. Most larger gifts are given from assets rather than income. Assets represent 91% of a person's wealth while gifts from income represent 9%. What is a major gift? To determine your "major gift," fundraising consultant, Amy Eisenstein, recommends identifying the top five donors in your computerized donor database ("a must for serious fundraising") and noting the range of their gifts, whether several $1,000 gifts by one donor or a $10,000 gift by another. Step Two is to determine an amount based on Step One. She says, "An appropriate level for a major gift is an amount where approximately 5 percent of your donors can (and will) give at that level." She adds, "Be realistic and yet optimistic when picking an amount. If you've never received a gift of over $1,000, then $25,000 is too big of a stretch. In that case, you should probably start with $5,000 or less." [63]

Let me re-emphasize, major gifts are the result of developing relationships with donors who may have previously given lesser amounts. And usually, those relationships are developed by trained development staff. Jerold

Panas says, "I believe that any organization with a budget over $5 million annually should have a full-time Planned Giving Officer. I find, however, if planned giving is shared in the portfolio, say with major gifts— planned giving is neglected like over-ripe cheese." [64] We have used 91% and 9% figures many times. Gifts from wealth may lead to much larger gifts than gifts from a person's income. 91% of wealth is in the form of non-cash assets, so without a planned giving program, fundraising is from only 9% of donor assets.

FUNDRAISING TREE

Thanks to my childhood wish lists and my parents' response, I learned that "money doesn't grow on trees." So, I'm obligated to show you that acquiring it from its true source may be illustrated by a "Fundraising Tree." Its trunk is the planned giving program, which grows from the roots of an organization's mission and values. Its branches are the methods that grow from the planned giving trunk. And its leaves are additional fundraising events and efforts that blossom along with or from the branches.

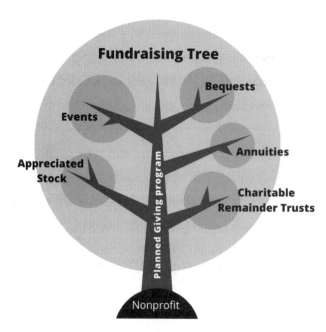

The giving landscape has changed—some of it by design and some by erosion. Fundraisers must keep in step or they will be out of the parade. Target marketing isn't just for big box stores and online merchants; it is for everyone who seeks "customers." For example, let's again visit how your nonprofit seeks gifts from women donors? *US Trust* found that "women are nearly twice as likely as men to say that giving to charity is the most satisfying aspect of having wealth."

- 64% of donations are made by women.

- 55 is the average age of widowhood in the US.

- Widows outnumber widowers 4 to 1.

- Women make 80% of all purchases.

- Women will inherit 70% of the $41 trillion in intergenerational wealth transfer expected in the next 40 years.

- Women give 3.5% of wealth to charity while men give 1.8% to charity.

In addition, the Silent Generation and Baby Boomers must continue to be a target audience for fundraising efforts. I believe that there at least 9 reasons nonprofits should appeal to older donors:

1. Their average donation is higher.

2. Their second gift rate is higher.

3. Their retention rate is higher (especially in monthly giving).

4. Their giving in event fundraising is higher.

5. Their chance of supporting another event is higher.

6. They have a higher lifetime value.

7. Their chance of putting you in their will is higher (and a higher chance of realizing it sooner).

8. Their chance of becoming a major donor is higher.

9. Their chance of responding to your communications is higher.

Interestingly, the dust hasn't settled on the Baby Boomers' financial journey. So, their giving cannot be considered a slam dunk. For instance, Baby Boomers. . .

- Have a "you only live once" mindset.

- May dip into their retirement money while still working.

- Are wary of taking risks.

- Annually spend $400 billion on consumer goods and entertainment.

- Spend $120 billion on leisure travel.

- Face rising costs of aging on a fixed income, including medical care and nursing home care.

- Support children and grandchildren education costs

The good news is that Boomers *will* be a prime source for investing in your nonprofit for decades.

- With $46 trillion in assets, they are the richest generation in history.

- From 2007-2061 they will transfer $30-$59 trillion through wills and estate plans.

- Spend 78% of all dollars spent online.

- Give nearly 50% of all philanthropic giving.

- Are 30% more generous than older donors.

I think there are at least three action steps to consider in building a relationship with Baby Boomers that will influence them to become donors.

First, notice them. For the most part, they can feel lost in a world of numbers and passwords and new technology and cultural change. Be for them. Befriend them. Be honest with them. Seek their counsel and let them know how you put it to work.

Second, involve them. Put them in the spotlight and make them feel valued. Put them to work in your organization. They have wisdom and skills that are invaluable.

Third, inform them. Keep them in the loop about your charity by adding them to your mailing lists. Make them aware of planned giving and financial management tools in a spirit of consideration and an atmosphere of enthusiasm. Appeal to their idealism as you share the vision of your nonprofit. Remind them that giving to a charity is a choice we have as American citizens and is a perfect way to see their money work while they are living.

MORE IMPORTANT

You may wonder why someone like me, who has raised money for the last 30 years, would author a book entitled, *It's Not About the Money*. The answer is simple: It's not about the money! I believe that there are many things more important. Spiritual health is more important than money; relationships are more important than money; physical health is more important than money. When we share our time and resources with others, we gain a greater appreciation of who we are and how blessed we are. Craig A. Dunn, Larry Moore, and Stan Toler said it succinctly in their book *To-*

tal Stewardship, "Prosperity is not having an abundance of money, goods, or time. It is enjoying God's presence and blessing in a right relationship with Him."

As I serve on the boards of Appalachia Reach Out (ARO) in Kentucky and Kinwell Academy in Indiana, I realize how much I have to be thankful for. I learned of young people who live in homes without water, heat, or electricity. I heard of a student who wouldn't use the laundry room of a facility because it would expose other students to bed bugs from the infestation in her home. That saddens me when I think of those who have so much and yet wrestle with not being content with what they have. Research shows that most wealthy people don't admire life's little pleasures as much as others. As great as money can be, it can lead to more stress, more work, and financial envy.

Americans should be grateful for our place of birth. Yes, our lifetime income correlates with where we were born. We get a head start on others. A person in America who makes more than $34,000 a year is considered to be in the top 1% of individuals in the world. I think people find it easier to give when they can see how others live. When I go to Florida each year, I know that I will pass homeless people who live near those with mansions. Fundraising programs connect donors with means to organizations and people with needs. And often those branches bring financial assurance to people who have *only thought* about intergenerational wealth transfers.

WILLS AND WON'T

Jeff Reeves wrote in *USA Today*, "According to a 2015 *Rocket Lawyer* estate-planning survey by Harris Poll, 64% of Americans don't have a will. Of those without a plan, about 27% said there isn't an urgent need for them to make one—and 15% said they don't need one at all." [65] Why do people fail to make a will? *One*, it forces them to think about death. *Two*, it is viewed as a costly process because lawyers are involved. *Three*, they do not recognize the value of their assets. Still others are ashamed that they haven't saved more money during their lifetime. Prospective donors must understand that if they die without a will, they are considered intestate. Normally under intestate law, the distribution of assets is pre-determined by the degree of relationship. Without a Will, they cannot choose their beneficiaries or dictate the executor who will manage their estate. Further, they can't reduce or eliminate inheritance, estate, or income tax.

- In Michigan, where recording star, Aretha Franklin reportedly died with an $80 million estate—and no will—a person dies intestate and the assets are divided equally among children. Franklin had four children, but not having a will opened the estate for others to claim they are entitled to it.

- Prince died with an estate estimated at $300 million—with no will. As a result, courts have been trying to sort out his legal heirs for decades.

- Frank Sinatra who had been married four times, had an estate worth more than $100 million but had cleared the protests in his will by stating that anyone who contested his will would be automatically disinherited.

Most of us are not famous or have funds equal to the people mentioned, but it remains important for all of us to get a plan in place. And, once a will is made it is important to update it every couple of years. (For example, my son who passed three years ago needed to be removed from my will.) Procrastination is the biggest enemy of estate planning. *Not* planning can lead to financial chaos and family disputes. Planning, on the other hand, can take advantage of economic opportunities—like the current highest estate tax exemption with the lowest death tax rate since 1997. (It is reasonable to anticipate an estate tax exemption decline and/or estate tax rate increase after the Tax Cut and Jobs Act expires in 2025.)

We must become more aggressive in planned giving programs. We know that only 5% of the US population has initiated a will or estate plan. We know that 70% of the gifts given in 2018 ($410 billion) were given by individuals. What does that mean?? We who are in fundraising must work smart. The average gift in planned giving is said to be $35,000-70,000 and could be even as high as $100,000.

PLANNED GIVING

As I have stated, my preferred planned giving systems/vehicles are Wills (Bequests), Annuities, Charitable Remainder Trusts, and Appreciated Stock. Let's review them briefly to see how they may fit into your fundraising efforts.

WILLS (BEQUESTS)

Wills and bequests are the most common form of a planned gift (90%). *Legal Dictionary* online defines them as "a gift of personal property, such as money, stock, bonds, or jewelry, owned by a decedent at the time of death which is directed by the provisions of the decedent's will; a legacy."[i] They include *charitable request*—gifts to religious, political, or social purposes, and reduce estate taxes owed on an estate; *demonstrative request*—gifts paid from a designated bank account or stock from a designated corporation; and *general bequests*—gifts taken from decedent's general non-designated assets. The donor may specify an exact amount, a percentage of their wealth or money left over after all obligations of the estate have been satisfied. The process is usually pretty straightforward. Learn more:

- Bequests are the major gift of the middle class.

- Of Americans who have wills (42%), 9% have included a charity.

- 70%-90% of all bequests are unknown until after a donor's death.

- The average age of someone making their first charitable bequest is 40-50.

- Women are more likely to give a bequest to religious, health or human services.

- Those without children are far more likely to make a planned gift.

- 1/3 of Americans are willing to consider a charitable bequest.

- Once a donor names a charity in their will, 97% of those gifts are never revoked, and 75% are never changed.

There are many benefits of giving to a charity through a bequest.

A. It ties the donor closer to a charity. The very act of naming it in a legal document is an indication of a donor's admiration and respect for the charity and its stakeholders. Jesus said, "Where your treasure is, there your heart will be also" (Matthew 6:21).

B. The act of making a bequest prompts the donor to consider other acts of giving—and opens their life to the promises of God's blessing. One gift can set in motion a lifetime of giving.

C. Making a bequest usually follows a donor's consideration of their overall estate. The bequest may start a chain of actions that will lead to financial security in other areas. Stephen Pollan and Mark Levine wrote, "Dying without a will is the ultimate abdication of personal control and responsibility." [66]

The influence of children on charitable estate planning is great (only 9.8% of donors who had grandchildren chose to make a charitable bequest, while 50% of those without offspring included a charity in their wills.). The number one reason people dropped a charitable bequest from their wills was that they became grandparents. For those who added charities to their wills, the decision came when they started making gifts to charity. One study indicated the importance of soliciting bequests from childless donors rather than using age or giving levels. Adrian Sergeant, Professor of Philanthropy at the Lilly Family School of Philanthropy at Indiana University, said that the wish to leave a legacy was a major factor in giving a bequest to charity. In addition, many who wish to "leave a legacy" aren't financially able to give during their lifetime, but through planned giving, they can give from their estate.

ANNUITIES.

Charitable Gift Annuities are a form of planned giving. A donor gives a larger sum of money to a nonprofit for a fixed annual income for the rest of the donor's life or in the case of a two-life annuity, a fixed income for both the husband's and wife's life. Depending on the type of annuity, the National Committee on Annuities generally sets an annuity rate that will provide the nonprofit with a 50% return on average. There are companies that sell annuities, but I like charitable annuities because the donor receives a charitable deduction upfront which can go against other tax liabilities. And, the charity is the benefactor of the gift upon the death of the annuitant.

Donor Search says a "gift annuity occurs when a donor makes an agreement with a nonprofit. Normally the charitable organization will set up a minimum amount required to initiate an annuity. Smaller charities may set $5,000 as the minimum while larger charities may require a gift of $50,000. The nonprofit then pays the donor an annual set income from that sum until the pay period ends (usually with the donor's death)." [67] Pollan and Levine cited the advantages and disadvantages of annuities. Their advantages:

- They are the only financial products in the world that can definitely provide a lifetime income.

- Fixed annuities provide a guaranteed income.

- Income paid out of an annuity is partly tax-free.

Their disadvantages:

- An annuity is only as certain as the financial solvency of the insurer that issued it. [For that reason, at IWU, we did not use the annuity as it was given but waited until the donor passed. That assured the donor that our organization would be able to honor the annuity to its full value. I have witnessed other charities who spent the annuitant's money and struggled to honor the annuity commitment.]

- The risk that one could die soon after buying one. [68]

CHARITABLE REMAINDER TRUSTS

As I have already noted, a Charitable Remainder Trust pays the donor a specified amount for life or a specified amount of time and is irrevocable. In the case of a trust, there are two primary trusts that are used, 1) *The Charitable Remainder Trust* pays the donor a specified amount for life or a specified amount of time and is irrevocable. 2) *The Charitable Lead Trust* provides payment to the charity rather than the donor for a specified number of years. At the end of the trust's term, the payment reverts to the donor or their designated beneficiary.

I recall a 91-year-old lady telling me that she only had $40,000 left in her estate but that she was giving it all to IWU upon her death. She was struggling to exist. In an effort to help the donor, I suggested that she give the $40,000 now for an annuity, the annuity would pay 11.4% and she would have that payment until her death. I have heard that people who exercise an annuity generally live 10 years longer. Of course, I have not verified that research—but she did live another 10 years, and IWU didn't realize the normal 50%, but I always loved the fact that I had compared her to the lady with a widow's mite.

Pollan and Levine call Charitable Remainder Trusts, "one of the secret wonders of capitalism." Julia Kagan, the former editor of *Consumers Report*, says it is "designed to reduce the taxable income of individuals by first disbursing income to the beneficiaries of the trust for a specified period of time and then donating the remainder of the trust to the designated charity. This is a "split-interest" giving vehicle that allows a trustor to make contributions, be eligible for a partial tax deduction, and donate remaining assets." [69]

APPRECIATED STOCK

In *Making Sense of Investing* by Edward Jones, the author says the appreciated stock is donated to a charity by re-titling shares in the name of the charity. "If you donate appreciated stocks that you've held for more than a year to a "public" charity—such as a religious or an educational institution, or an organization that does medical research—you can typically take a tax deduction for the full fair market value of the stocks, up to 50% of your adjusted gross income for that year." [70]

Kimberly Lankford, a contributing editor for *Kiplinger*, advised, "Giving appreciated stock you've held for more than a year is better than giving cash. If you donate stock that has increased in value since you bought it more than a year ago—and if you itemize deductions—you can take a charitable deduction for the stock's fair market value on the day you give it away." She also said it's better to sell a losing stock first and give the cash to a charity—deducting a capital loss and an itemized charitable donation. [71]

MANY BRANCHES

Of course, the "Fundraising Tree" has many branches—and affiliate branches. Equally important in building the annual fund is the *direct mail campaign*—normally 3-4 letters each year. I found that letters can speak to the heart of donors and result in additional funds for the organization. Howard Taylor, a friend of mine whom we hired shortly after my coming to IWU and is now a consultant and writer of fundraising letters, has taught me several things about direct mail. I have found them to be successful and have passed them on to others during my years of working with charities. He never used a one-page letter but rather encouraged two pages. He wanted a lot of white space, and room to write a P.S. in cursive on the second page. 90% of the readers read the P.S. first and for that reason, I always put an Ask in the P.S. Most of our appeal letter used anecdotal stories of students or stories that faculty shared because of their emotional impact. Another friend, who wrote fundraising letters for a worldwide religious broadcast said when he planned the letter, he envisioned the "average listener" (according to studies, a 50- to 60-year-old woman) reading the letter and wrote to her—including stories of compassion and need. The best audience for gift planning and a legacy Ask is in the annual fund or direct mail fundraising effort.

- Direct mail indicators such as recency, frequency, and average gift are a great way to cultivate planned giving and legacy donors.

- Individuals with a strong link to a charity show a strong link to legacy giving.

- Board members should be considered prime prospects for a legacy gift.

- Women seem to make more bequests to a charity (53%) compared to men (47%).

- Despite tax incentives, the desire to support a charity is based on the use of the gift. A desire to support the charity appears to be the major motivation of most donors.

In direct mail to IWU donors, I always selected a premium that would accentuate the message of the letter and often increase the size of the donation. I also used premiums that were compatible with the mission of the institution—finding that Bibles are excellent premiums that bring donor response. I used a bonded leather Bible that could be embossed with the institution's logo or seal. Now, years later, it makes my day to see alumni or friends of the University carrying those Bibles to church. And those Bibles include an outstanding promise regarding planned giving: "The generous will prosper; those who refresh others will themselves be refreshed"

END OF YEAR

Many organizations are not aware that 34% of giving comes during the last 3 months of the year and that 12% is given during the last 3 days of December. People are more charitable during those times. It's said that 74% of people will give during the holidays. Have you ever wondered why you receive so many requests for a donation from local charities during the last 3 months of the year? I encourage all charities to gear up for personal visits and a robust direct mail campaign at the end of the year. There are three basic reasons people are giving during the last 3 months. 1) Tax benefit, 2) The spirit of the season, 3) Charities are making appeals. Robin Cabral gives steps to segment major donors and to ask for their support in a calendar year appeal:

1. Be sure that your reply device mirrors the messaging of the direct mail appeal.

2. Ensure that even your reply device includes your mission statement and, perhaps, even a donor impact statement.

3. Save your organization money by having the donor place the stamp.

4. Include monthly, quarterly or any recurring donation options on your form.

5. Include a section where donors can make gifts: "In honor of/In memory of…"

6. Ensure that all email captures are "permission-based." For example, "Yes, I would like to receive periodic updates from the organization."

7. Include a check-off box to encourage volunteering.

8. Have a check-off box where folks can indicate their interest in making a planned gift.

9. Always include contact information.

10. Consider adding suggested amounts that mirror the copy of your direct mail appeal letter. [72]

GAP CALLS

Another fundraising strategy that I use at the end of the fiscal year and calendar year is what I call "gap calls." A gap call is generally made over the telephone but for larger donors who have gapped the charity for more than $5,000, I recommend a personal visit. I generally develop a spreadsheet for the last 5 years and see who has been giving on a consistent basis. If they

Gap Calls	2016	2017	2018	2019	Gap
John Doe	$300	$500	$1,000	$200	$800
Mary Smith	$1000	$500	$500	$100	$900
Sue Jones	$100	$200	$400	$0	$400
Ralph	$5,000	$5,000	$5,000	$0	$5,000

have given $1,000 each year but only gave $200 this year, they have gapped your charity $800. Failure to fill that gap is a loss to your charity and may result in additional losses in the future. At the end of the fiscal year, I encourage the donor to continue to be a member of named giving club, such as the Trustee Citation, President's Club, Dean's Club or Community Club at whichever amount is their level of giving. Many of your donors have simply forgotten to send in a donation and need a gentle nudge. Others may need to air a grievance and they are back on board with future giving.

LANDMARKS

Fundraising trees serve as landmarks, pointing people in the desired direction. Trees are comprised of two main types, "deciduous" (trees whose leaves change colors and shed—like changing fundraising methods) and "evergreens" (trees whose leaves remain throughout the year—like traditional fundraising methods). But both have a variety of looks and strengths and possible use. Let me share some fundraising tree landmarks that I've noticed along a 30-plus year career in raising funds for nonprofits.

WEALTH AND GIVING

- The wealth transfer is top-heavy, with 20% of affluent families transferring 88% of the wealth.

- Wealthy donors give to places where they volunteer their time.

- Donor response varies according to methods (Example: direct mail: 1-5%; telephone: 25-40%; personal contact: 75-80%)

- Many widows and widowers wish to honor their spouse through planned giving.

- The most common candidates for bequests to charities are older people who never married and have the means to make a generous gift.

- Giving from income is an entry-level, low-emotion gift; giving from assets is a more mature-level, high-emotion gift.

- Most bequest donors will have been donors for three or more years when making a decision on the will.

- The size of gifts during life is not an indication of the size of a bequest.

- The majority of bequests come from wills that were executed within seven years of death.

- Giving through charitable bequest usually grows during a recession, unlike the annual fund.

- Search your database for "Miss" rather than "Ms." "Miss" tends to be older ladies.

- Research shows 80% of current donors would recommend your organization to others – the "referrals" are 3 times more likely to give.

GENERATIONS

- The entrepreneurial Baby Boomers' giving is more like investing than charitable support. They want to know the return on the money they give.

- 1 in 3 Millennials is depending on inheritance to achieve financial security.

- Millennials prefer giving to smaller organizations.

- Boomers have saved $152,000; Gen X: $66,000; Millennials: $23,000.

- 1/4 of healthcare spending comes in the last year of life.

- Many older people who are making end-of-life plans are still in the generation who like to get direct mail.

FAMILY AND CULTURE

- 39% of Americans who have been married since 2010 are married to someone of a different faith.

- 42-45% of 1st marriages end in divorce; 60% of 2nd marriages end in divorce; 73% of 3rd marriages end in divorce; the most common age of divorce is 30 years.

- Nearly 2/3 of people under 30 who have never married say they would like to get married someday.

- Women now outnumber men 100 to 85 in receiving a college education.

- 80 of the wealthiest people in the world collectively share the same amount of money as 3.5 billion people.

% Leaving Charitable Bequests	Size of Estate
4-5%	All Americans
20%	$3.5 - $10 Million
28%	$10 - $20 Million
40%	$20 Million +

None of those "landmarks" are earth-shattering, but they are indications of the wide range of experience in the lives of those we serve. A college business major interviewed a wealthy older man for a class assignment. "How did you make your fortune?" he asked. The exquisitely dressed gentleman said, "I made it during the Great Depression." The astonished student replied, "During the Depression! How did you do it?"

The man said, "I was down to my last nickel, so I invested it in an apple from the fruit stand. I spent the whole day polishing it, and at the end of the day, I sold it for a dime." "Totally awesome!" the student replied. "There's more," the man said. "I invested that dime in two apples, polished them all day and sold them the next day for twenty cents. I continued that and by the end of the month, I had nearly a dollar and fifty cents."

The student looked puzzled. "You made a fortune selling apples during the Depression?!" "Not exactly," the man replied. "The next month, my wife's father died and left us two million dollars."

"Giving is the secret to a healthy life.
Not necessarily money, but whatever a person
has to give of encouragement, sympathy,
and understanding."
– John D. Rockefeller

CHAPTER 9

Donors Once, Friends Forever

S ome of my best friends are donors I had never met. I have loved my work for many reasons, but one of the best has been developing new relationships into lasting friendships. I have had the privilege to work with some of God's finest folks! Their faith, their vision, and their generosity have been lessons in my own money management and spiritual growth. Donors aren't just donors. They are people with a multitude of life experiences that have shaped and motivated their lives. I love sharing life with them, whether in an office, in their home, at a restaurant, or on a tour bus.

Most people pick a charitable organization with whom to have a relationship because of a connection with their family or community. My relationship with the Green family of the Hobby Lobby organization started nearly 20 years ago when I visited them in Oklahoma City. Because they closed their local store in Marion on Sunday, I was intrigued and called for David Green. He agreed to see me, and we met on several occasions. During that time, I discovered he had a grandson who was a high school senior and was looking to attend a Christian College. Dave's son, Mart gave me a call one day and said they were flying into Indianapolis and asked if I would be available to give them a tour of the Indiana Wesleyan University campus. They had been in Panama working on a movie that was to be released called "The End of the Spear." It features the story of the missionaries who had been killed by the Auca Indians years ago. Mart and his son, Tyler, arrived on campus and after a tour and some discussion, the decision was made, and Tyler arrived on campus that fall for his freshman year. I continued to make trips to Oklahoma City to meet with Dave and Barb Green. During one of the visits to Oklahoma City, I asked Dave if he would speak at an IWU fall commencement. It involved his speaking three different times, but after much consideration, he accepted the assignment—and did a wonderful job. His inspiring presentations greatly enhanced the lives of our Adult and Professional students.

Shortly thereafter, I asked his wife, Barbara, if she would consider becoming a member of our Board of Trustees. She said that she would consider it and made the decision an item of prayer—and a fleece. The fleece was that if Tyler came back for his sophomore year, God would be in her serving on the board. Barbara was not aware of it, but the following August I made weekly calls and regular visits to the Admissions Office to see if Tyler had enrolled and when I saw the name Tyler Green on the enrollment roster, I made a call to Barbara Green saying, "Guess who the newest member of our Board of Trustees is?" She replied "I wondered how long it would take before I received a call. I will serve." And for 15 years, Barbara served on the board and poured her efforts into making IWU a quality Christian university. All of that, to illustrate that relationships with those who support a nonprofit require time—and the donor is given an opportunity to give advice and share their ideas.

RELATIONSHIPS MATTER

Sue Vineyard said, "When we recognize that a better word for fundraising is 'friend-raising,' we open limitless doors to creativity in support of our causes." Everyone involved in asking someone to commit resources from their estate must have an established relationship with them. When I meet a prospective donor, I just assume that we will be friends. Every relationship is enriched by knowing more about the other person. Each generation has a unique set of values that motivates them to participate. One misconception of planned giving is that fundraisers can wait until a donor reaches age 65 before talking about it. As mentioned, it takes seven years to cultivate one planned gift. All ages, particularly adults 40 years and older, are prime candidates for a planned gift. This is another reason for having longevity of service in the advancement staff. Relationships that yield results in giving have been cultivated over time.

Many nonprofits have given their planned giving staff wider responsibilities. Gift planners are no longer just a specialist in one area but assume many other activities. For instance, professional financial advisors in the for-profit area are helping individuals make many of their planned giving decisions. This has caused nonprofits to shift in emphasis toward major gift fundraisers. Also, the change in the tax laws has reduced tax incentives for planned giving. Smaller charities tend to look for a generalist who can advise in planned giving but also understand the importance of marketing and building relationships with donors.

I am a strong advocate of an organization's marketing a planned giving program to their constituency. This is where I would cultivate individuals who participate in the annual fund and keep those same individuals aware of their need to become a planned giving donor. *Cultivate, cultivate, cultivate*, using both functions simultaneously. Inform potential donors of your nonprofit's success. When an individual donor expresses an interest in a planned gift, ask them if they have someone they work with regarding their financial plan. Rarely do we utilize our organization's attorney until their attorney is involved. Today, most people have access to information regarding estate planning.

DOORWAYS OF OPPORTUNITY

Death is very common—but obviously, that isn't "Breaking News." The Bible says we are "appointed to die." Though it is common, a person's death is rightfully noted with interest and respect, so much so, that obits and memorials are popular features in print or online news. Many print and online publications have a "People We Lost This Year" column, spotlighting the passing of celebrities or other members of a community. No one is immune from dying yet it seems like everyone is concerned with prolonging life. We diet, exercise, and get medical checkups to "push the death envelope." Our life expectancy has increased and causes us to think we have more time to make the wealth transfer decisions—but many haven't. Missionary martyr, Jim Elliot once wrote, "When the time comes to die, make sure that all you have to do is die!"

Maybe some people haven't made transfer decisions because they're hesitant about prioritizing their life, and asking such questions as: "What would I start doing differently?" or "What loose ends would I tie up?" or "How could I become more in tune spiritually?" As financial advisors, the questions are doorways of opportunity. The Apostle Paul described his work, "A great door for effective work has opened to me" (1 Corinthians 16:9). The Great Handoff is a large, open door! We have a chance to offer "holistic" planning that equips clients with spiritual as well as financial options. In that same Scripture verse, he notes, "there are many who oppose me." People who seek to close doors of opportunity often have "a story" from past experiences. They remember that death often brings the worst along with the best in family relationships. And often the source of the "worst" is centered on property issues.

After my wife's mother passed, and her father remarried, I remember how my wife and her sisters were hurt when they discovered that most of the family keepsakes were sold in an auction or disposed of in a dumpster. Without communicating with other family members, heirloom items like a beautiful pump organ and other antiques owned by her grandmother were gone. The importance of communication is paramount. Because of poor communications, my wife and her sisters never formed a fondness for "their father's second wife" and had negative feelings toward their father for allowing the loss of their mother's and grandmother's keepsakes.

How could that happen? A study by Fidelity Investments revealed that the number one reason parents fail to discuss their estate plans is that they don't want their children to count on a future inheritance. Most people know they should discuss money matters with their children, but many are concerned with distributing their estate equally. For example, how do you split a Florida condo between two children who have equally fond memories of the place? Another door of opportunity for financial advisor professionals! One way to have a good conversation about an estate is to leave the numbers out of the initial conversation. Talk instead about a modest way of living, what is important, how money should be spent, realities about the estate, and the importance of making a living.

I remember one couple who lived a very modest lifestyle; in fact, on each visit to their home they would be picking up sticks to keep the house warm, and on one occasion taught me true frugality. I had lunch with the couple, and the wife told me that I could freshen up while she heated the can of "SpaghettiOs." I proceeded to the bathroom to freshen up and when I flushed the commode, red rust entered the toilet bowl. As I left the bathroom she was smiling and said, "I noticed you flushed the toilet," to which I replied, "I'm sorry, was I not supposed to?" She then demonstrated the "proper method" with a ladle she kept by the bathtub. I had noticed the milky water in the tub, but I soon realized that old bathwater was being repurposed. Dipping the milky water from the bathtub into the commode until the toilet flushed, my hostess said, "That is how you flush the toilet and save electricity by not running the pump."

Some would say that was extreme, but I would say that people from her generation knew the importance of pinching their pennies. The couple had experienced the Depression firsthand. I admire their thrift and the fact that several colleges profited from it by receiving $2.7 million in bequests when they passed. I'll admit that I have not adopted their electricity-saving procedures, but I cherish their hearts for God. Many adults would do things differently if they could go back a few years. They have regrets about their saving and spending patterns. The lesson? Americans may be watching their diets but neglecting their financial well-being.

Fundraisers have a unique opportunity to bridge the gap between what *should* be done and what *can* be done. Financial vehicles and instruments are already in place to make the intergenerational wealth transfer smoother than most would imagine. Of course, that depends on the knowledge and skill of a financial consultant and the cooperation of family members. Planned giving offers the best of all "financial transfer" worlds. Nonprofits need resources that prospective donors already have. And those donors are looking for mutually profitable ways to help meet those needs. But programs need knowledgeable administrators. And donors need caring

> *"Help others without any reason and give without the expectation of receiving anything in return."*
> – Roy T. Bennett

counselors who know about programs and recognize their value beyond a bank account or a trust fund. Three decades of working with fundraising and contribution methods have given me an understanding of what *can* be done. But the knowledge that pleases me most, is what I have learned about *how* it is done—through relationships with people who want to make a difference beyond their lifetime. Caring for donors and prospective donors is the intersection where methods and management meet friendships.

Often as fundraisers, we have the pleasure of visiting with people who become close friends. That was the case with Lyle and Nell who live in Dallas, Texas, but also have a home in Branson, Missouri. An invitation to their place will make you think you're on vacation, not just visiting with friends. Our relationship with them resulted in an invitation to my wife and me to spend several days in Branson. Boat rides on Table Rock Lake, playing golf on a Jack Nicklaus course, attending nightly shows to see performers like Kenny Rogers, Pat Boone, Andy Williams, and Bobby Vinton was a dream come true. But the greatest times were playing table games and talking about the blessings God had given each of our families. My relationship with Lyle and Nell started when their former pastor shared their names with me. He mentioned that he had given their names to other fundraisers, but they were never contacted. I assured him I would make a contact, and about a month later made an appointment to have dinner with them in Dallas.

I found them to be very pleasant to talk with and invited them for a campus visit. During that visit, I asked Lyle if he would be willing to serve on our Pace group which involved two meetings per year. He consented and during that first year while serving on the President's Advisory Council on Excellence, he committed to give $1.1 million to assist the University. This gift and his service to IWU was certainly a tremendous asset to the University, but the friendship that my wife and I established with the couple has continued, as we talk by telephone or make an occasional visit.

DONOR CARE

Nonprofits and their advance staff focus on donor care in three areas:

- Identifying who they are and what they might be able to give.

- Cultivating a relationship with them that will result in both their interest and their investment.

- Asking them to commit monies from their resources to the annual fund through a major gift or planned giving.

IDENTIFYING DONORS

Prospective donors are closer to your organization than you might think— geographically, relationally, and philosophically. They are people within your web of influence that identify with your organization's values and mission but may not know how to cooperate in it. The fundraiser is responsible to link those resources with an organization's values and mission.

When I work with nonprofit boards, I often try to help the organization uncover new prospects by using a "Give Me Five" exercise. While working with a Christian school in Merrillville, Tennessee, I met with approximately 150 PTA members and asked them to "Give me five!" I explained that it wasn't a physical "high five," but rather a financial one. And since I was introduced as a professional fundraiser, I imagine they weren't sure whether the "five" would be five dollars, five-hundred dollars, or five-thousand dollars. So, I assured them they wouldn't need to guard their purses or wallets. I handed them a 3 x 5 card and asked them to complete the card with the names of five people who would give to the Christian school because of their relationship with them. I suggested that they consider individuals in their church or community who:

- Own their own business.

- Retired early.

- Own a winter home in a sunny climate.

- Travel extensively.

- Own commercial property, apartment buildings, or farmland.

- Are known in the community for their charitable giving.

	Amount of Ask	Relationship	Assist with Ask
1. John	$1,000	Neighbor	Yes
2. Mary	$10,000	Business Associate	No
3. Sue	$25,000	Banker	Yes
4. Bob	$50,000	Uncle	Yes
5. Don	$100,000	Grandpa	No

The group immediately responded, and names began to go on the cards. As I collected them, I promised the group that I would respect their wishes if they chose not to be involved in the Ask. Later, a husband and wife came to me and shared their card, asking me to look at the top line of the card, which had a name and a $500,000 amount to ask for. They asked me if I recognized the name and I replied that I did but had not called on him. When I asked how they knew that person, the husband said they were friends, "My wife played basketball at Rice University in Houston, where she went to college, and our families vacation a week together each year."

Until that time, I had not used the "Give Me Five" approach, but since then, I have used it many, many times—and each time new donor prospects were identified who could be cultivated and asked to give a gift. I always suggest that the friend of the prospective donor be the one who makes the Ask. (It is more difficult to turn down a friend who is asking.) Some think it might destroy a friendship if they ask. My response is that if it destroys a friendship, they weren't that good of friends. Others are hesitant to be involved in the "Give Me Five" because they think of fundraising as a "tin cup exercise," i.e. *begging* for money. So, I try to help them understand that *asking* is simply providing a donor with the *blessing* of *investing* in the lives of others.

CULTIVATING DONORS

Two great questions for fundraisers: "Where are the donors?" and "Which donors are likely to include our nonprofit in their estate plan?" In my book, *It's Not About the Money*, I talk about the largest gift we ever received from an individual, $10 million. The donor, Art, was a 90-year-old humble man who loved the Lord. But he was very lonely after the death of his wife, Mary. Thankfully, he met and then married the "second love of his life," Nell. They were surprised and yet humbled when we proposed naming a student residence hall after them. And for years, it became their place of ministry. They would show an interest in and build relationships with the students, regularly taking one or more out to eat. I remember a joyous occasion when the students held a 90th birthday party for Art in that residence hall, expressing their love and appreciation to him and to his wife. Nearly three years later, Nell died. Art was strong in his faith, but the loss of his beloved was a tremendous heartache.

In an effort to help him cope with the loss of his wife, I volunteered to stay at his home overnight. Before bedtime, Art and I had a special time of reflecting on the blessings of his nine-year marriage to Nell and made plans to go out for breakfast in the morning. At about 1:30 a.m., Art (who was always properly dressed) came into my bedroom dressed in a suit and tie and ready to leave for breakfast. He had misread the clock, so I assured him we would leave in about five hours, and he spent the rest of the night in his recliner. He was a generous donor who also became a dear friend. I was privileged to be there for him during some difficult times, and after his death, I knew that our advancement team had been a blessing to him as he, in turn, blessed us. Connecting with donors calls for establishing a friendship with them. There aren't any strict rules or procedures that must be kept, just showing interest, being helpful, being available, and showing kindness and courtesy in the name of the Lord. Let's zoom in for a closer look at those characteristics.

1. SHOWING INTEREST

You've probably heard the expression, "It's lonely at the top." In other words, those who have climbed the ladder of success vocationally or financially often suffer from loneliness, even when surrounded by people. Sometimes "1%" people are viewed as aloof or unapproachable until a situation (crisis or otherwise) reveals their approachable side. Never has our culture had greater tools or methods to bring people together than now, yet a US surgeon general said that loneliness in America is a "serious public health concern." Dr. Shannia Ali, a licensed mental health counselor, wrote in *Psychology Today*, "In the last 50 years, rates of loneliness have doubled in the United States. In a survey of over 20,000 American adults, it was found that almost half of the respondents reported feeling alone, left out, and isolated. Further, one in four Americans shared that they rarely feel understood, and one in five people believe they rarely or never feel close to people." She further quotes a *Cigna Loneliness Index* study, "Only about 18 percent of participants believe that there are people with whom they can communicate." [73]

Fundraisers wear many professional "hats," but when it comes to dealing with people and cultivating their interest in an organization they represent, "professional hats off" is the best policy. I have noticed that once human kindness reaches out to human loneliness amazing things happen. All major gifts or planned giving amounts given by donors started with one person making personal contact with them. When I meet people "for coffee" often very little coffee is consumed. The meeting isn't about coffee. Coffee is just a "decoration" in the setting whose real purpose is to connect with another person on an emotional level. You might call it "highly caffeinated caring." (And I might add, people are quick to know when "decaffeinated caring" is substituted!)

Donors of any economic status are *persons* first and everything else is secondary. They are persons with homes and families and concerns and wishes we all have on different levels. When I am invited into a home, one of the first things I do is to make a "sight scan." My eyes move around the room to see items on display. Those items, including photos, collectibles, trophies, plaques, or unique furniture pieces are dear to the heart of their owner. They are great conversation starters and bridges of connection. Effective fundraisers focus on the details. One or more details noticed and commented on could influence the direction of a prospective donor's interest and investment.

Each donor visit culminates in completing a "call report" which highlights important information discovered during a visit. It includes items like hobbies, important facts about the children, interests, health issues, college attended, wintering in Florida, etc., and I often note information that requires follow-up. I have had donors wonder how I remembered their wife's cold or a recent stay in the hospital. Believe me, it is not because I have a great memory; it is because I pay attention to details included in a call report.

2. BEING HELPFUL

John Edmond Haggai said in his book, *Paul J. Meyer and the Art of Giving* "The right handling of relationships might be termed an 'investment of influence,'" and illustrates it with a quote from Newell Hillis.

"Friend shapes and molds friends. This is what gives meaning to conversation, oratory, journalism, reforms. Each [person] stands at the center of a great network of voluntary influence for good." [74] Said another way, each *fundraiser* stands at the center of a great network of voluntary influence for good. Who you are and who you represent is never more important than what you do or what your organization does for others. But a giving spirit is easier "caught" than taught. How can we expect donors to make sacrifices of time or resources that we are not willing to make ourselves?

I remember Luella. A single lady in her seventies, Luella purchased rental homes ostensibly for income, but my guess is she rented them just for the company of the renters whom she visited regularly. Her loneliness was at the core of her business venture. For instance, Luella insisted that her tenants pay their rent in person. Those "porch meetings" with a tenant were a way for her to interact with people—and escape the emptiness in her life. She had attended IWU for a brief time and continued to have feelings for the University. Knowing that I made it a priority to visit her regularly. Our conversations were mostly about her church—the focus of her life. I also helped her with financial matters, including some bad loans she had made, and getting her books in order. Because of her age and health issues, I even assisted in collecting money owed to her. Advancement staff also helped her with her finances by setting up annuities that gave her a life income.

Luella had talked about a scholarship fund in honor of her minister father, so we helped her fulfill that dream as well. Always grateful for my help and the help of our staff in seeing to her well-being and protecting her finances, Luella made provisions for the ongoing scholarship funds to help others. Upon her death, IWU received $85,000 to grow the scholarship fund for future ministers. Being helpful was our investment, being generous with her estate was hers. Helpfulness is a great way to cultivate the interest of donors. They must know that you care about them as a person of value before they will consider the value of giving to your organization.

> *"Talent is cheap; dedication is costly!"*
> – Michelangelo

3. BEING AVAILABLE

Raising money wasn't easier in the days before the Internet and cell-phones. 21st-century technology has at least partially closed the communication gap. But for many older donors, the gap is still there—despite AARP deals on smartphones with oversized buttons. Keeping donors informed is still a challenge, but one that must be conquered. I firmly believe that cultivating prospect or donor interest in the workings of your nonprofit is a pre-requisite to asking them to invest in it. Nonprofit blogger, Ann Green, wrote, "It's crucial that all your communication is donor-centered. Sending a newsletter or update that just brags about your organization doesn't show your donors you care about them." She also gave good advice about "little deals" that are really "BIG DEALS," like this one about communication pieces: "It may not seem like a big deal to you to address your donors as 'Dear Friend' instead of their names, but it matters to them." And stressing the importance of a good database, she notes, "Monitor your database to make sure you have accurate records. Misspelling a donor's name and sending duplicate mailings may also not seem like a big deal, but if you can give your database the attention it needs, you're showing your donors you care about them." [75]

If we are to communicate effectively with prospective donors or donors who have already given, we will need staff who are skilled communicators AND listeners to enrich the cycle. Good listening is a valuable fundraising skill that often gets lost in the messages about good communications. I have heard that the reason God gave us two ears and one mouth is to emphasize listening skills. Fundraising and campaigning professional, Jonathon Gapsas, lists some availability reminders that include communication tips. Allow me to use them as main points.

1. Set personal and staff standards for the response. Every successful organization has policies and procedures in place. For the planned giving staff those policies might include turnaround times between inquiries and response, the kinds of data that are included in a database, and matching communications methods with responses. Consistency is key to the image of the program and the reputation of the staff.

2. Train staff on types of giving. Do your fundraisers know the difference between a "charitable trust" and an "annuity"? They must be aware of all types of giving if they are to make recommendations to those who decide to donate through a planned giving program. As I've said, I prefer to incorporate trained specialists from notable financial institutions on boards and committee—and in training staff.

3. Ensure absolute clarity in communications. Make sure everyone is on the same page in messages to prospects and donors—including the organization's statement of purpose or mission. And make sure that all communications are matched with the prospect or donor's understanding and experience. Effective communication is on a person-to-person basis, never from one person "talking down" to another.

4. Respond in the same way you were contacted. Types of contacts reveal the preferences of those who make them. Often older prospects or donors are more comfortable with a phone call or "snail mail" than email or texts—though people are changing with the methods of the times. The bottom line is to never assume a response method.

5. Keep promises. Nothing says inefficiency like promising one thing and delivering another. If you say, "I'll call you tomorrow" make sure you do. If you set a meeting time and place, try to be the first one to arrive. Promising copies of papers should result in copies in hand. And promised letters should actually BE "in the mail" if you say they are. Your trustworthiness is a reflection of the organization you represent.

6. Focus on donors rather than your organization. More than likely, your nonprofit is already on a prospect or donor's A-List. So "promotion" should be secondary. "You" is a friendlier word than "Us" or "We." And, "How can we help?" sounds better than "Here's what we've done."

7. Personalize communications. People are proud of their name, no matter how difficult it is to spell or pronounce. Use it freely and often. Most will read letters from nonprofits they are interested in, but their attention is "grabbed" with handwritten, personalized sidebars or P. S. messages.

8. Focus on values, not cost. Prospects or donors with resources are usually more interested in the return, not the cost. Emphasize the *value* of service over its cost.

9. Provide ongoing training and resources for staff. Learning opportunities are skill-sharpening events. Communicators should also have the best equipment affordable to function effectively. Staff restricted to using "*IBM Selectric*" typewriters will find it difficult to produce communications fit for people living in a digital world.

10. Produce inspiring rather than functional communications. Letters are used to inform, encourage, and inspire. The difference is in the story. Even a form letter can move a heart with compassion with an identifiable storyline that is true and powerful. Speak to the heart in your communications and the mission of your organization will stick in the reader's mind.

11. Produce reader-friendly mailings. Communications should be audience-focused. Include paid reply envelopes, use a standard font (minimum 12-point), gain attention with a headline, and make the appeal more than once. For older audiences, use a larger font with an increased amount of white space and avoid color backgrounds.

12. Don't over-promise. Communications are advertisements in a sense, but they should not promise things that are unbelievable or unavailable. Tell your story in the first paragraph and start your appeal in the second. And make the "close" personal. [76]

If all of that seems like a full plate, "Wait! There's more!"—and it's all about balance. In John Edmund Haggai's book on entrepreneur and philanthropist extraordinaire, Paul J. Meyer, he says of Meyer, "He has achieved a level of efficiency that permits him to spend almost a third of his time in nonprofessional activity (family, church, or private hobbies). And half of his directly related work time (time, energy, and resources he devotes to running his businesses and philanthropy) goes to future planning." [77] What I learned in my "degree" from the "College of Hard Knocks" is now readily available in print and online. Taking care of a fundraising business means continuing education, not a diploma event. And it's learned from "boots on the ground."

4. SHOWING KINDNESS AND COURTESY

In his book, *More Than a Hobby*, David Green talks about the necessity of helpfulness and courtesy in his stores. "We cannot dismiss the idea of greeting our customers, being friendly, and staying pleasant. Every question deserves an answer. Whenever we hear, 'Where is such and such?' our people normally escort the customer to the precise aisle rather than just pointing 'Over there.'" [78] People who give to your organization are people who have decided to "open the books" on their life and finances. It is a personal commitment that must not be taken for granted. A "Big Thank-You" doesn't have calculable dimensions, but in many cases, it may look smaller than it seems—like the proverbial message on an automobile's rearview mirror. A donor's "Big Thank You" should be in ACTUAL SIZE—or LARGER. And, we cannot assume the major gift or planned giving experience is over once there are signatures on an agreement. In every case, that is just the beginning. Kindness and courtesy are ongoing.

An article by Claire Axelrad in *Bloomerang* online reported a shocker, "Research shows the average nonprofit in the U.S. loses 77% of donors after the first gift! Overall donor retention is only 45%. By the time you've added a new donor a majority of your previous donors are out the door." Then she gave action steps to approach donor retention as "a purposeful journey rather" rather than a "wandering endeavor."

- The gold standard, and what people expect, is a prompt and personal mailed **thank you letter**. Not a "canned receipt." (Add a personal, handwritten note—elevating it from 'canned' to special.)

- Immediately send an **email** to donors who give online. (Attach a brief video or photo that shows how the gift will be used. And let the donor know that a letter will follow.)

- Make a **phone call**. Before or after "the letter" call the donor and express your gratitude. (Phone calls have the most lasting impact. A study said those who were called within 48 hours of their gift gave 42% more after 14 months.)

- Send a **Thank-You video**. (As simple as recording a message on a phone camera.)

- Create a **"landing page"** on your website. (Include compelling image or video that shows a gift's impact.)

- Post on **social media**. (Personalize and link a video showing their gift in action.)

- Send a **text**—especially to younger donors. (Text within 48 hours of the gift.)

- Mention donations and donors in your **newsletter or blog**. (Include noteworthy donors or donations.)

- Add an "honor roll" to your **annual report.** (And "this was only possible because…" references.)

- Host a donor-honoring **event.** (Include donor names throughout the program.) [79]

Smith and Clurman concluded, "Over 60 percent of consumers in each generation agree that 'most of the time, service people they deal with for the products and services they buy don't care much about their needs.' Half or more of every generation… would be willing to pay at least 10 percent more with a guarantee of better service." [80] No matter your job title or classification, if you are a fundraiser for a nonprofit, you are—and always will be—in the "service industry." Your donors or donor prospects have 1.5 million registered nonprofit organizations from which to choose. You alone could narrow the margin to ONE.

"Dear God…help me to gradually open my hands and to discover that I am not what I own, but what you want to give me."
– Henri Nouwen

CHAPTER 10

The Ask

"He who snoozes loses" is a common expression that serves as a painful reminder. It all started with a very bright and beautiful girl in my high school Algebra II class. She could answer math questions almost as fast as Mrs. Lutz could write the problem on the chalkboard. I watched her with interest for several weeks and months. Our brief conversations in the hallway highlighted my day. And when it came time for our class party, I envisioned her as the perfect "date" to accompany me to the party…but she went with another boy. Why? Perhaps because I didn't ask her. I was afraid she would say "No." I guess one reason the other boy took her to the party was that he refused to "take 'No.' for an answer" and accompanied her to the party while I played "second fiddle in the orchestra." My failure to ask left my whole dream sequence incomplete.

The same principle applies to fundraising. *People give to people. People give to people with a cause. People give to people with a cause who ask.* Those three statements are simple. Most of us know the first two, but the last one results in positive action from a prospective donor. Millard Fuller said, "I have tried raising money by asking for it, and by not asking for it. I always got more by asking for it." In one sense, fundraising is all about asking in faith and receiving in thanksgiving. But we need to look under the hood and check out the mechanics. I think there are six questions that should be answered in our mind before we make the Ask:

1. Why do we ask?
2. Who should we ask?
3. What should we ask for?
4. When should we ask?
5. How should we ask?
6. What happens if they say "No"?

I wonder how often we as fundraisers have made calls on prospective donors who seem to have a positive feeling toward our charity, we have a special relationship with them, and we know they have an interest in our wellbeing. They have given us small gifts through an event or a direct mail campaign. Yet we fail to make the Ask. I recall a situation where a donor named Jim had given me $200 to $500 on a yearly basis for several years. His donation came as part of our county's Scholarship Day, and he would receive a certificate of participation he would display in his businesses. However, this day was different. I met him at his request, and we started with the usual small talk—but it suddenly shifted to something I hadn't anticipated.

Jim informed me that he had sold his 15 "Handy Andy" convenience stores and assumed that I would be calling on the new owner. But then he said something startling: "Ask me for a gift." What a change in roles! People I call on normally know why I am calling and are ready for the Ask. But

Jim caught me off guard. He repeated his original statement with greater intensity, "Ask me for a gift!" Although this was the first time a donor had "invited" me to make the Ask, I quickly gathered my wits and said I wanted him to consider a gift of $250,000. No sooner had the words come out of my mouth when he replied, "You got it!"

Oh, how I wish every donor had that spirit and was willing to share their good fortunes with others. Later, I asked Jim how he would like to designate the $250,000. He then told me the story of his teacher in high school who had taught his brother Jack and him to play the violin. He wanted to use the money to fund a scholarship for students pursuing string instruments and to build a stronger string section in the instrumental music program. Jim named the scholarship the "Lloyd DaCasta Jones Scholarship." Each time I attend an orchestra concert at IWU and hear the string section with their beautiful harmonies, I am reminded of the day Jim said, "Ask me for a gift."

1. WHY DO WE ASK?

Asking for a gift can be intimidating. How will the person react? Will it prove that I have been on target in my cultivation of this donor? It has been said that "a ship in harbor is safe. But that is not what ships are built for." Fundraisers must display and thrive on boldness. Most good fundraisers that I know have three speeds: fast, faster, and still faster. But why are they in that mode—and why do they ask?

There is an interesting story about Andrew Carnegie that emphasizes how important it is to make the Ask. Each year when representatives of a museum would call on Carnegie for a gift, he would give them $5 million. One year while they were making the annual ask for $5 million, Mr. Carnegie expressed his frustration, "I continue giving each year, but no one steps up to match my giving. I carry the burden for your annual support year after year. This year, it has to be different. I will only give $5 million if you get someone to match it." The board members left terribly disappointed. But weeks later they came back, and to Mr. Carnegie's surprise, reported that they had found someone to match his gift. "Wonderful! I'm delighted!" he responded, and added, "See, I told you if you asked you would find someone. Who is it?" They replied, "Mrs. Carnegie."

I can't stress enough the importance of an Ask. The biggest reason people do not give to your charity is that you have never asked them to. That has been proven time and again in my travels to colleges, Christian schools, churches, and nonprofits across the US. Oh, they may think they are asking when they say, "Will you consider a gift?" But that is only what I call a "hint" rather than an Ask. I have observed over my 30 years of working in fundraising that one of the greatest reasons, if not the number one reason, a nonprofit is not successful in raising funds is not because it asks too often or asks at the wrong time or asked for the wrong amount. The reason: they haven't asked in the first place! People at all income levels want to feel wanted; they want to change the world by making an organization in their community a better organization—and in turn, make their community a better place. They want to improve someone's life so that one will bring improvement in the lives of others. And they are deprived of that opportunity because no one has asked them to help.

> *"Giving is the master key to success, in all applications of human life."*
> – Bryant McGill

As fundraisers, we must come to grips with the fact that asking people to become major donors is as much a benefit to them as it is to the organization we represent. By asking their help, we *help them* realize their potential. Giving to others is a pleasure that makes people happier in the process. Researchers have found that giving to charity is an altruistic behavior that activates regions of the brain associated with pleasure, and releases endorphins which produce a positive feeling. Giving has also been linked to the release of oxytocin, a hormone that induces feelings of warmth and connection to others. It is through giving that we enrich our lives and the lives of others.

Giving to a charitable cause also encourages others to give. It inspires our network of friends and family to follow our lead and give to charities that are important to them. For example, sharing the importance of giving with your children will help them grow with a greater appreciation for what they have and to respond to the needs of others. Giving feels good, so why not spread the good feeling. A wealthy and wise man once said "When God blesses you financially, don't raise your standard of living. Raise your standard of giving." Throughout history, wealthy family members have been influenced by their parents to give and care for those less fortunate.

Making the Ask can help to bridge the ever-increasing gap between those who can afford to give and those who can't—something that organizations face when they meet budgeting shortfalls. In 2015, the top 1% made more than 26 times the income of the other 99%. Jeff Bezos, owner, and CEO of Amazon became the richest person in America, with a fortune of $150 billion, at the same time the median net worth of all Americans was $68,828 per household.

The top 10% of Americans control more than 70% of the nation's wealth, while young professionals with student loan debt have a negative net worth.

- Student loan debt has increased by 160% since 2004, and Millennials have taken on three times more debt than their parents.

- American Millennials have an average net worth of less than $8,000, which is less than other generations their age.

- During the last decade, Millennials have been paying 65% more for their education than their parents and nationally student loan debt is at $1.5 trillion.

For the rich, wealth provides security while the middle class uses its wealth for emergency expenses or retirement. The ask is more opportunity than imposition. It unlocks the *mind* to explore unknown benefits of generosity. It unlocks the *heart* to think beyond self. It also unlocks God-given *resources* that can be used for His kingdom purposes. When Elijah the prophet asked the poor widow gathering sticks to give bread to him (1 Kings 17), he promised that her flour and oil would never run out. This teaches four positive benefits of proactively asking for a gift.

First, asking tests the donor's priorities. Spiritually, it causes them to consider whether they are storing up treasures in heaven or keeping them for security on earth. The Ask gives the donor an opportunity to respond in faith with a generous gift that could have eternal implications.

Second, asking can trigger God's blessing in the life of the donor. In the story of the prophet Elijah, the widow who gave the bread went from famine to feast in one act of faith. I believe that in heaven, donors will thank you for asking—and may even wonder why you didn't ask for more.

Third, asking teaches the one who asks to trust God. In today's world, the widow in Elijah's day might have been relegated to a direct mail piece rather than a personal Ask. And some fundraiser might have missed the experience of seeing God using someone to supply a need.

Fourth, Giving is transformative. It not only changes the conditions of need for organizations and the people who receive its benefits, but it also transforms the giver. How many times have you seen someone's life transformed by serving on a mission trip or donating time to a local shelter? You'll hear something like this, "Wow! I never knew what a blessing! I expected to give to them, but they gave back to me!"

Money represents the physical and emotional investment we put into our jobs. Money can give us options, power, security, or pleasure. But unchecked, its influence can grow until it strangles a person's soul. As a fundraiser, we can help to loosen money's hold on people by encouraging them to give it away—and spare them from the consequences of falling for money's sinister game.

- Giving helps them to know they're doing something significant.

- Giving makes their lives more meaningful.

- Giving makes them feel connected to something bigger than themselves.

2. WHO SHOULD WE ASK?

The answer to the question of who we should ask may seem too simplistic, but it is true. Anyone or any organization that has a passion to use their God-given blessing of resources and shares the ideals and mission of your nonprofit is a prospective Ask. There are several predictors that a charity will be considered for a planned gift:

- **Involvement.** - The donor has attended activities or functions at the charity.

- **Loyalty.** - A family member has been involved with the charity.

- **Frequency**. – The frequency of gifts from the donor or their consistency in giving over several years. Most major giving and planned giving began as annual gifts. Persistence, not rapid persuasion, is vital to the success of planned giving. Research shows that 78% of planned giving donors gave 15 or more gifts during their lifetime to colleges named in their will.

- **Age.** - Most donors over 50 years of age should be considered a prime target for a planned gift.

- **Education.** - What is the prospective donor's educational attainment? We know that the more education one receives, the greater their giving.

Opportunities sometimes arrive in packages with an unexpected return address. The old saying, "Ask for money, you'll get advice. Ask for advice, you'll get money" reminds me of the time I visited with a retired couple who had not given to IWU, but both had served as college professors and administrators in other institutions. At that time, we were going through a North Central Association study that was required every 5-7 years. I asked the couple if they would have any interest in reading our report and giving it their critique since they had experienced it several times—essentially asking for their advice. They helped with the report, but the next year the college received a gift of $10,000 from them, and they continued their support for several more years!

Peer pressure does have an effect on giving behavior. In small group settings, we generally send two volunteers to make a gift request. You may ask, "Why two volunteers?" Because asking for money is difficult and this gives the group more confidence? No, because a second observer will generally increase the size of the gift by 40%. When presenting to a small group, people in the group are more likely to respond. Also, with two people representing the Ask, you are more likely to get a genuine response. It is called accountability.

However, large Asks should be made on an individual basis. It is a mistake to ask the entire board in one setting to make a commitment to a capital campaign, particularly, if some board members have a greater capacity to give. Again, people who give because of peer pressure (e. g., other

Board members) are less happy about their donation and many have given to avoid shame rather than to support a cause.

3. WHAT SHOULD WE ASK FOR?

We often look at external conditions. Generosity is not necessarily connected to a person's appearance or actual net worth. Some who are wealthy-looking—or actually are wealthy—may be woefully uncharitable in giving. Generosity isn't a look; it is a character value. It comes from a person's heart in response to a felt need. Often, we are hesitant to ask someone to give who "doesn't look" like they have the means to give. I heard of an elderly lady who was successful in real estate holdings and could afford most anything. However, when she went shopping, she would put on "shopping-clothes"—worn looking, hand-me-downs with an obvious button or two missing, scruffy shoes and a hat that looked like a Minnie Pearl reject. She explained, "I don't want those store people to think I have money!" And almost every time, the ploy worked—getting her a bargain without a "sale" sign in sight.

We are helping people connect their passion to our cause. What are some other causes they support? What do they have a passion for? What is their history of giving? It is important that we always ask for specific amounts when making an ask. We were involved in a capital campaign in Westerville, Ohio when I received a call from the individual who was monitoring the campaign. The steering committee had identified individuals who would need an Ask and the amounts that were suggested for the person to be asked for. They discovered that many donors who were identified for $50,000 or $100,000 asked had only given $10,000. After a visit to Westerville and a few questions of the volunteers, we discovered that the volunteers were asking for range gifts. If the contact report said the prospective donor should be asked for $50,000 or $100,000, the volunteer was asking for $10,000 to $50,000 or $10,000 to $100,000, respectively. It didn't take long to realize that human nature being what it is donors were choosing the lower number of the ask.

After a short strategy meeting, we shared with the volunteers that if they feel more comfortable asking for a range gift and the contact report indicated a $50,000 or $100,000 Ask that the range gift request is for $50,000 to $100,000 or for a $100,000 Ask a range gift Ask would be for $100,000 to $125,000. It was surprising to the volunteers that some people gave more than what they expected. Make certain that you always ask for a specific amount. Indicators to determine what to ask for: past giving, 54%; capacity to give, 28%; a formula, 12%; and peer giving, 5.3 %.

4. WHEN SHOULD WE ASK?

As I've said, cultivating donors for an Ask takes time. I have witnessed institutions who have pursued cultivating a prospective major donor for 2-3 years. But it has been my experience that after two or three visits with a prospective donor over a 6- to 9-month period, the fundraiser has a good idea whether the person is a prospect for an Ask. Remember, the first gift will not be the largest gift the donor will give, and the charity can't receive another until the first gift has been given.

Before one makes an ask it is necessary to educate the prospective donor about your organization. Success in the asking process requires that the project be relevant to the donor. There needs to be an emotional appeal with a sense of urgency. The fundraiser must display a passion for the cause. Many fundraisers reach a point where they are not really asking; they are simply "apologizing" for the ask—or even begging.

"No gift is too small."

"Anything you can do will help the cause."

"Would you consider giving a gift?

Instead, the Ask must be grounded in the "absolute necessity" of a need.

And I must add, sensitivity to the person, place, and circumstance is the difference between a true professional fundraiser and a wannabe. Let me illustrate it rather crudely. If you owned a shop selling fine china collectibles, you might want to put a sign on the front door that says, "This store is off-limits to robbers and raging bulls!" The fact is, one raging bull can do more damage in one minute than a team of robbers could do in a week.

To be a successful fundraiser you must have an honest heart and a perceptive mind. I recall an incident a few years ago when I met with a wonderful Christian friend. I had scheduled the breakfast meeting to ask him for a major gift. As I approached the table where he was seated, I noticed that he had been crying. In fact, the cloth napkin that he had been using was saturated with tears. I immediately asked him what was wrong. He responded that he had just received a telephone call from his daughter indicating that she had filed for a divorce. I can assure you that at that moment my fundraising hat was off. He was devastated and needed a friend to share his pain. As we talked, he told me that he would give all the money he had if he could put his child's marriage back together.

I assured him that we could meet at another time and that our meeting was not as important as his family. "No," he said, "I know why we are meeting today and I would like you to go ahead with your presentation." I continued my presentation with an Ask for $4 million. Without hesitation, he said that he could do $3 million for the project and revisit the request at a later time. I will admit that on that day with the circumstances as they were an Ask was probably not appropriate.

Some would speculate that if I had rescheduled, the donor would have given the full amount; however, a busy businessman who has many distractions may have considered other requests and diminished the amount to an even lower figure. It does emphasize my point that if you wait until everything is perfect, the Ask may never be made. We must act with sincerity and sensitivity. And the affirmation of this "God-planned moment" resulted in another meeting and his gift of $2 million.

The most important facet of fundraising is relationships. Some of my greatest friendships are those I developed during those fundraising years. They don't ask me how much money I have raised, but how my son or daughter is doing. "What about the granddaughter that is playing tennis?" "What college are your grandchildren attending and what major did they decide to pursue?"

Often, as in the case of Brooks and Wanda Fortune, they simply call and ask if I have time to stop by and have a piece of apple pie? The answer is always "Yes." Wanda would say, "How about some freshly made apple pie?" While Brooks would say, "Wanda, could you please bring my checkbook?" Relationships that last beyond a gift are the best kind. Sometime before, I had discovered that the Fortune Foundation located in Indianapolis provided grants to Christian causes and decided that we would submit a proposal for funding. The proposal was for $10,000 to fund a nursing scholarship at IWU.

After completing the proposal, the Foundation requested that it would be submitted by mail. Because of the close proximity to my home in Marion, I decided to hand-deliver the proposal. After a telephone call, I discovered that the Foundation office was in their home. I rang the doorbell and to my surprise, was greeted by Mrs. Fortune. "My name is Wanda," she said. "Would you like to meet Brooks Fortune. I had done some research on the Foundation and knew that he once held an executive position at Eli Lilly and Company. I replied that I would be delighted to meet him, and Wanda ushered me into their living room where Brooks was seated.

I introduced myself and handed him the nursing proposal. He said the timing was good and that the Foundation Board would be meeting to review proposals in about a week and that I would be notified the following week about the Foundation's decision.

He then asked if I had time to talk. Since Brooks was in his 80's, Wanda suggested that I sit near him so he could hear. This was my first encounter with the Fortunes, but they were very open and extremely hospitable. Brooks asked me about my family and my job at IWU. For nearly two hours, we shared about our families, our work and our love for Christ. I can't recall a visit that went so well and that I enjoyed more. About a week later we received a letter from the Foundation that the nursing scholarship for $10,000 had been approved. Little did I know that my initial visit would turn into a friendship that would continue for several years and continues with Wanda yet today. I was a guest in their home numerous times. During one of our visits with the Fortunes, they indicated that they spent the winter months in Florida and if I had an occasion to be in Florida during the winter that they would like to take me to lunch or dinner. On my next trip to Florida, I scheduled a lunch meeting with them. As I entered the living room, Brooks was seated on the couch, evidently in preparation for our meeting. He had been reading thank-you letters from nursing students who had received his scholarship. I noticed he was visibly touched. As tears ran down his cheeks, he said, "Terry, I want to raise that $10,000 scholarship to $20,000." Sometimes fundraisers get blessings without making an Ask.

When Brooks died, IWU President Barnes and I were asked to participate in the memorial service. Several weeks passed, and I received a telephone call from Brooks' son, Dr. John Fortune, telling me the $20,000 scholarship for the nursing program that we had been receiving would be terminated with his dad's death, but because of the friendship that we had developed, a Lead Trust had been developed and we would be receiving a check for $422, 000 to be added to the Fortune nursing scholarship fund. Dr. Fortune wrote a gracious letter:

> Dear Terry,
>
> As you know my father named Indiana Wesleyan University as one of the beneficiaries of his Charitable Lead Annuity Trust. Included is a check for $422.80.30. My parents were always thrilled to support the nursing program at Indiana Wesleyan University. I am sure they would have wanted this bequest to be directed to the scholarship fund. Thanks for all you have done over the years to welcome us into the Indiana Wesleyan University family. We look forward to seeing you again soon.
>
> Sincerely, John B. Fortune, MD
> President, The Brooks and Joan Fortune
> Family Foundation

A relationship that had started several years ago in the living room of the Fortune home had culminated in several thousands of dollars of scholarship aid for needy nursing students who attend IWU in perpetuity. First visits are important and making that good first impression can help your charity for years to come.

Warm-hearted conversations have heartwarming results. What do you share with prospective donors before making an Ask? It is always good to give a positive report on the fiscal integrity of the organization. People like to know that their gift is being handled by an organization that is experiencing financial success. We must always give donors a reason to want to support our organization. Most donors want to maximize the impact of their gift. And during my IWU days, I would talk about the stability in leadership—since both the president and I had a long tenure.

5. HOW SHOULD WE ASK?

The 3 most important areas to consider when making an Ask are

1. Relationship,

2. Planning,

3. Process.

RELATIONSHIP

Even before we make the Ask, some "givens" must already be in place. All relationships—including those with prospects or donors—begin with a good first impression. Only in extreme situations, do we ever get a second chance to re-purpose that impression, but even then, the first sticks like Super Glue in the mind of the other person. In fundraising, our initial appearance will cause the prospective donor to form an opinion of us and the organization we represent. Our goal is to make a positive first impression that will cause the prospective donor to want to know us better. When I think of people that I enjoy or want to establish a relationship with, I look for people who will enrich and add to my life. It is the same in donor-fundraiser relationships.

Jenna Goudreau wrote about first impressions in Harvard's *Business Insider*, "People size you in seconds, but what are they evaluating?" She quotes Harvard Business School professor, Amy Cuddy, who says our first impressions are based on two traits: 1. Can I trust this person? 2. Can I respect this person's capabilities? "If someone you're trying to influence doesn't trust you, you're not going to get very far, you might even elicit suspicion because you come across manipulative." [81]

Donors recognize a fake. As a fundraiser, be genuine. Experts say that within seven seconds of meeting a donor, they form an opinion of what that person is like. Are they a potential threat or can they be trusted? The initial impression you make will cause the donor to filter future behaviors to confirm their initial opinion of you as a fundraiser. Research has found that it may take up to six months of regular contact to change a person's initial impression.

Since appearance is important, make a special effort to look sharp. Exercise good posture, sit up straight, display good body gestures—all of which give clues to your attitude and mood. You are always more attractive with a smile. Oftentimes a firm handshake is a memorable first impression. We may think it is judgmental or unfair of a person to draw a negative impression of us because our shoes are unpolished or the crease in our suit is uneven, but that is their gauge of our personality or abilities. If you are calling on an older person, it would be advisable to get rid of the piercings or cover tattoos. When I served as Superintendent of Schools, I recall cautioning new teachers that I could not dictate their personal attire in the classroom but, because of their age and only being a few years older than some of their high school students, it would be advisable to have the students see them in a professional manner, in the way they dressed.

PLANNING

One strategy that I recommend when making an ask of a major donor is to have the organization's president, CEO, or executive director as part of the asking party. Oftentimes, if the ask involved a particular department of the University, such as teacher education, nursing, ministry, etc., I would try to include the head of that department. This person should be able to answer most any question posed by the prospective donor about their department. Having an executive as part of the Ask indicates the importance of the visit and adds credibility to the presentation. The person who makes the Ask is generally the person who has been the most closely associated with the cultivation process. Who would the donor have the greatest difficulty giving a "No" response to the request?

I also recommend having two individuals present for an Ask with a clear understanding of job assignments during the Ask. Including a third person to the asking party can oftentimes be cumbersome and sloppy. With two involved in the Ask, one can share the vision and the other make the Ask. I always recommend the use of two when volunteers are being used.

> *"For it is in giving that we receive."*
> – Francis of Assisi

Why? Accountability. The most common mistake made on a visit to make an Ask is that it isn't made. They may hint at an Ask or spend time talking about the organization they represent, but may never get to the reason for the visit. Another area of concern when making an Ask is the lack of good research, and as a result, asking for too little. There have been times, when making Asks for a charity other than my own that during the conversation, I discovered the donor had capacity above the agreed-upon-amount and it was necessary to raise the amount of the Ask during the visit. We need to challenge the donor.

When I make an Ask, I generally try to move to the front of my chair, with my hands free to make appropriate gestures. I tend to use my hands to express enthusiasm and excitement for what I am sharing with them. On occasion, I have had a donor who remarks, "You are really into this project" or "I really appreciate your enthusiasm." I want the donor to know how important the mission I represent is to me. I want my donors and prospective donors to know that I have something to offer that has value.

When asking for money, you make yourself vulnerable. You lay down your pride and let others know you have a need. They can say either "Yes" or "No" to your request. I remember making calls early in my fundraising career. I thought,

- "What do these prospective donors think of me as an individual?"

- "Does it appear that I am begging and dependent on their generosity?"

- "I am asking, asking, asking. Is there a chance that I could be offending them?"

These types of questions may race through your mind as you share the organization's mission. However, with each Ask your confidence level grows and you will feel less vulnerable. As a Christian, working with a Christian organization, I chose to believe that God was giving me a spirit of self-control and boldness. And, as I kept asking, I realized that the best way to conquer the fear of asking is repetition. I was building confidence with each Ask. Every donor is different, which makes every situation different. With every Ask, you define how much you need, why it is needed, and the amount for which the donor will be asked. As that relationship develops in trust, you may invite the prospective donor to an event onsite, to participate in an activity or event. For instance, I have invited prospective donors to share their expertise in a symposium or activity on campus. I have also asked a successful business owner to share their business expertise with a business class, knowing the experience would give them a positive experience and a feeling of involvement.

PROCESS

During a meeting with a donor, try to determine their interests. It is important to hear their stories. Use what you SEE as a starting point for what you SAY. Furniture, collectibles, paintings, sculpture, or photos are clues to what they value, and make good subjects of conversation in initial visits. This small talk will allow you to transition to a discussion of your organization's mission and eventually to the Ask. One of the best ways to get your prospective donor to share information is to ask questions. People like to share information about themselves. The better you make them feel, the more likely they are to share and develop positive feelings toward you. See if you share any commonalities like college, restaurants, sports teams, hobbies, etc.

Personally, I have found that the more visits I make, and the more Asks I make, the more competent I become in my ability. In almost every visit the donor will know the reason for your visit. They usually understand your role with the organization and therefore know you will likely make an Ask. When I am getting ready to make it, I demonstrate excitement with my presentation. I generally move to the front of my chair, with my arms free and demonstrating my love for the organization I represent. My goal is to help the prospective donor gain appreciation and excitement for the organization. For you, once the relationship is established—and ongoing—and the need is presented, you might ask for a small gift. This will generally give you some indication of whether the individual is interested in your organization. The next step would be to ask for a reoccurring gift (often at a larger amount), followed by an ask for a major gift, and finally a request for a planned gift. Start by getting the donor involved and progress to a giving level that will be of real benefit to the charity.

In seminars that I conduct, I often refer to the late Jerold Panas, who dedicated more than 50 years of his life to fundraising and authored more than 20 books on the subject. He said that to have a successful Ask, 55% will be based on appearance and 38% will be based on voice inflection. Most of us have heard the adage, "It's not what you say; it's how you say it." It is the same in the Ask. The way you deliver your words is of paramount importance.

When making an Ask, always present it as a question, not an open-ended suggestion. And, make certain to include a set dollar amount for the donation. The donor does not get the opportunity of setting the amount. If you fail to provide a concrete amount the donor will offer a lower figure than what you were going to suggest. The question requires a response of either a concrete "Yes" or "No." For example, "Would you consider a gift of $25,000 to provide scholarships for students in Grant County?" NOT, "A donation to the Grant County Scholarship fund would be helpful" or "I would like for you to consider a gift to the Grant County Scholarship fund."

Once the Ask had been made, it is the donor's time to make a decision. Stop talking. Be quiet and wait for a response. Allow the donor time to respond. The response may be "Wow that's a lot of money! You must think that I have more money than I do" or "Let me consider it. I need time to speak with my family" or "You certainly present a good cause. Let me make this a matter of prayer." As fundraisers, we often think we need to convince. We repeat the Ask and go on and on; but we need to just *stop, look, and listen*. Give the donor time to think. A failure to respond immediately by the donor does not mean they are going to respond negatively but are trying to think of a way they can respond positively to your request. They are trying to process how the gift will fit into their finances.

I remember calling on a very wealthy lady in Florida. After making an Ask for $500,000, the room became silent for what seemed an hour but, was closer to 30 seconds. Finally, the lady responded with "Wow! That's a lot of money." I responded gently with "That's only $166,667 for 3 years." She quickly said, "I can do that." Remember, even a "No" is not the conclusion of your Ask. We must master this art of closure to be successful.

Once the Ask is made, the ball is in their court. They, not the fundraiser, control the response. Making fundraising Asks may feel unnatural, awkward, or even scary. But knowledge and practice can make a person comfortable making an Ask.

Let's summarize by noticing the stages to an Ask.

1. Your first Ask should not be for money. Ask the prospective donor to visit your organization. Take them on a tour or ask them to volunteer their time or services. (Volunteers have worked many hours coordinating mailings for both the advancement and admissions departments saving them thousands of dollars in labor costs. Not only do we profit from their time, but most become donors as they get involved.)

2. Ask for money after the person has had a non-monetary involvement.

3. Ask them to introduce you to their network of friends.

4. Ask for an increased gift or recurring gift.

5. Ask for a major gift or a capital campaign gift.

6. Ask for a planned gift.

Although receiving a gift may or may not follow, I have found this outline to be very workable during my years as an advancement officer. Also, here are some practical tips for the Ask:

• Smile early and often.

• Stand or sit tall.

• Sit toward the front of your chair and lean into your ask.

• Don't cross your arms. Be physically accessible.

- Use good voice inflection and speak with volume.

- Express gratitude. Thank them for the visit.

- Be curious. What do you see in the room, office, donor's bookshelf?

- Make intentional small talk and show an authentic interest in the donor? What about their kids, vacations, work projects, likes, hobbies?

- Give compliments.

6. WHAT HAPPENS IF THEY SAY "NO"?

If you haven't received a "No" response to an Ask lately, there are two things I suspect, 1) You are only working with low-hanging fruit or, 2) you are not asking often enough. I would agree that there is nothing worse than receiving rejection after making a major gift request. War stories of fundraising rejection are probably the reason many people are afraid to be involved in it. Rejection is an inevitable part of fundraising. I always expect a "Yes," but I'm like the attorney in the courtroom who may receive an unexpected response but is prepared to deal with it. When I work with organizations who are struggling to raise major gifts, I tell them the most important metric to achieving success in fundraising is the number of asks made. I will agree that success is based on the level of experience of the fundraiser, length of service with the organization and portfolio potential but the greatest measurable factor will be how many asks have been made.

Good fundraisers are intuitive. Top major gift officers trust their instincts and listen to their intuition. If a donor has a problem identifying with the project, we must be flexible, prepared to offer alternatives. It may mean extending the period of time or giving to a scholarship effort rather than a brick and mortar project. In addition, our experience has been that donors are more willing to give when the project gets closer to the fundraising goal. Donors gain greater satisfaction when they know their gift will help the charity cross the finish line. I have visited with major donors who offered a challenge of the last $250,000 or $500,000 to complete a campaign. They realize that by giving the last portion the project will be successful, and their gift will bring the project to fruition. Good fundraisers can turn a "No" into a "Yes."

After receiving a "No" response, I ask the donor if I may ask a couple of questions. Assuming I have asked the donor for $100,000, I would first ask them if I asked for too much. If the answer is "Yes," I ask them what amount would have been appropriate. Again, assuming they say "$50,000," I will accept the $50,000 and thank them for their generosity. Then, I will ask if the timeline for meeting the pledge was extended for two years would they consider the other $50,000. If they respond that it was not because of the amount of the Ask, I would ask if the project was not of interest to them. In other words, does the proposed project not fit in their area of interest. "Would you have another area that you would prefer? I know we asked for softball field dugouts, but it sounds like you would be more interested in helping fund scholarships for the ladies' softball team. That is certainly a major need!"

If neither of the other questions gets a positive response, I would ask if the timing is not right. Perhaps they had mentioned during our visit that their stock had taken a hit or that the business was in a slump period, I would say, "What if we were to revisit this proposal in 30 or 60 days? Would you be better prepared to make a decision at that time?" This process normally helps the fundraiser appraise the reason for the "No" but it also can help turn the answer to a "Yes." A majority of people give because they think their donation will make a difference. Research has found that 85% of charitable donations came as a result of being asked.

Most of my large gifts (over $100,000) have come from individuals who are classified as from either the Silent Generation or Baby Boomers—individuals ranging from 65-90 years of age. One thing I have found in working with this age group is that often they do not respond to you because they didn't hear your Ask. I can't emphasize this point too much: elevate your voice. Make it easier for them to hear. There have been times when I arrive home after addressing older adults all day, and my wife will say, "You don't have to talk so loud; I can hear you!" So, I guess good habits in one situation can create problems in another.

There are other ways to improve the possibility of a "Yes" answer to your Ask. As time-consuming as it is, continuing to build your relationship with the donor is of utmost importance. It will require face-to-face meetings, learning more about their likes and dislikes, finding out what organizations they are currently supporting, and continuing to express kindness and service.

Social media standout, Michael Stelzner wrote about neuroscience and marketing, how people make decisions. He interviewed 30-year fundraiser Tracy Trost and asked what causes people to take action. Trost said, "Most of the decisions we make every day are based on what we believe, and most of those beliefs are based on things we were taught before we were 10 years old. Most of those decisions aren't based on fact; rather, they're based on what we subconsciously believe about something. We react versus respond." And then he quoted from Robert Cialini's book, *Influence*, and his six principles of persuasion:

1. Reciprocity – The obligation to give back to others for services received.

2. Scarcity - Point out what is unique about your proposition and what they stand to lose if they fail to consider your proposal.

3. Authority - People follow the lead of credible, knowledgeable experts.

4. Consistency - People like to be consistent with the things they have previously said or done.

5. Liking - People prefer to say yes to those they like. We like people who are similar to us, we like people who pay us compliments, and we like people who cooperate with us towards mutual goals.

6. Consensus - People will look to the actions and behaviors of others to determine their own.[82]

Donor cultivation can also be fun. I remember with fondness fishing trips on Lake Michigan with a donor named Tom—catching our limit of lake trout almost every day and hearing about his life as a POW during World War II. Or, boating and riding on jet skis, and playing golf with our friends Lyle and Neil. Or, golf outings with my good friend, Larry Maxwell. There really IS fun in "fundraising"–plus the bonus of lifelong friendships.

My experience in fundraising also helps me look for red flags of warning. *First,* if we're not careful, we will tend to deal with the urgent rather than the important. *Second,* if we spend most of our time and energy strategizing, we will have less time to focus on production—plus, of course, the things that matter most: emotional and spiritual health and family relationships. *Third,* we need to narrow our focus and work on fewer goals, deciding which activities are most important and how to implement them. Working smart is a lot better than "just working." Fundraisers must focus 75-100% of their time on the Top 10% of donors if they will have any long-term success. Mother Teresa said, "Yesterday is gone. Tomorrow as not yet come. We have only today. Let us begin."[83]

POSTLUDE

Things I Cherish Most

Ididn't receive a lot of earthly treasures from my parents, but what I did receive, I cherish most. My parents were poster children for the Silent Generation. Their core values were "traditional"—discipline, self-denial, hard work, respect for authority, and financial and social conservatism. Slow to embrace new products, they saved money and saw retirement and leisure times as a reward for hard work. Dad fought during WWII in North Africa, Sicily, and the Italian campaign. He felt honored to serve his country and had great admiration for such Generals as George Patton and Mark Clark. I remember many times when we attended a sports event, tears fell down his cheeks when the "Star-Spangled Banner" was played.

UNDERSTANDING THAT HEALS

I didn't understand Dad's emotions until later. I learned that during combat in Italy, he recovered a company machine gun while under counterattack by the Germans and received a Bronze Star Medal for heroic achievement, as well as the Purple Heart. Many of his fellow comrades fell during the campaigns. Out of 193 men in his company, only 37 returned. It's one thing to MEET a person, and another to KNOW that person, to look past how they appear into who they really are. A person's behavior mirrors the soul of their experiences. My clients and their donors became my forever friends because the more I learned about them became the reason I loved them.

FAITH THAT TRANSFORMS

Religion is a paltry quantity compared to the wealth of a personal relationship with God by faith in His only Son, the Lord Jesus Christ. My dad discovered that during wartime combat. He was totally unchurched but had memorized John 3:16. He recalled that one day under enemy fire, he held onto the stake of a grapevine and quoted that verse as a prayer of faith, and accepted Christ as Savior.

Though his new-found faith didn't erase the old fears or anger brought by flashbacks of his combat years, it helped him see how dependent he was on the Lord. The classic saying, "God has no grandchildren," never depreciates. Dad and Mom couldn't transfer their faith to me, but they did what they could to help me find my own. Scripture says we could gain the whole world and lose the most valuable thing we have: our soul—the eternal part of us that is never satisfied until it rests in God.

VALUES THAT COUNT

Values aren't valuable because of what they bring to us; they are valuable by what they make of us. Values were the seeds my parents sowed in our hearts. They kept us going when our income slowed almost to a stop, and helped us discover what really counts when there wasn't much to count!

They put a "stick-with-it" in my spirit that helped me accept the immediate but work to make it better.

Mom taught me to be a provider. She canned vegetables and always made sure the potato bin in the basement was full. But for Mom, work was never more important than family. I can remember getting home late from baseball or basketball practice and Mom coming out of the barn with the milk bucket, pouring it into the metal milk cans. She would try to have our nine cows already milked to save me from having to change my clothes to join her in the milking parlor. That was Mom. She worked tirelessly for the Munday clan, never asking for or expecting praise. We all knew we were dearly loved.

Eating out would be an anomaly. But occasionally after Wednesday night prayer meeting at the church, we would stop for a 25-cent ice cream cone at Eckstine Dairy Queen. Values are the wealth of life. Everything else comes and goes with the tides of time. Who you are, comes from what you believe.

EFFORT THAT BLOSSOMED

Our family wasn't Ozzie and Harriett perfect, Dad struggled with war memories and often reenacted them. He also carried over his Army disciplines in correcting us. And sometimes Mom had to mediate a lesser punishment for something Dad thought deserved a greater. But he would ask our forgiveness when he crossed the line, and we began to understand the motives behind his emotional boil overs. We knew we had to make a "Capital E effort" to make it all work together. And we put that effort into our work, whether it was slaughtering chickens or butchering hogs or bailing hay.

I remember the scratches on our arms from bailing and stacking hay— almost like temporary tattoos. But the chores resulted in great memories and childhood entertainment. For example, we would compete to see how high we could stack hay in the wagon—while the tractor was still pulling it to the barn.

MEMORIES THAT ANCHOR

When we finished Dad's to-do list, Mom had another one waiting. She would draft us to help her work the garden, teaching us to do our part to make sure there would be vegetables to last the winter. I'm sure money—or its lack—was, heavy on the hearts of our parents, but they didn't seem to worry about it—at least in our presence. And what do I remember most of those days? Fun times mixed with days of "hard labor." Going for a swim in the river across from a large hayfield near us. A rope swing hanging high in the tree that made it seem as much fun as sliding down a water slide in one of today's mega water parks—especially on a hot afternoon after a hay bailing.

CONTENTMENT THAT SATISFIES

Our parents couldn't have afforded a family membership in the local fitness center, even if there had been one. But Dad could nail a basketball hoop to the side of the garage and Mom would join us or watch us shoot baskets or play a game of H-O-R-S-E. And Dad could help us dig a pit to play horseshoe in the side yard. What we had, kept our attention away from what we didn't have. That wealth still grows interest in the bank of my heart. I am so thankful I learned how to be content. Spontaneity is a gift that your family will always treasure.

EDUCATION THAT LASTS

Downtime on the farm was limited, but Sundays were a mandatory day of rest. Since we didn't have TV, reading was "the great option" to pass the day. That gave us two things: a reverence for the commandments of God's Word, and a love for reading and learning. They carried me during my days as a teacher and coach, and through 30 years in fundraising and advancement for a large and influential Christian university.

FORTITUDE IN LOSS

With clues given by my parents, I finally found the grace of God that saved me and called me to surrender my life to Him. And the grace that formed my own spirit still reigns in the home my sweetheart, Linda, and I established. But how little did we know how much of it we would need! Several years into our marriage, after two daughters, Lynn and Shelli, were born, we were blessed with a third daughter. Heather brought a new joy to our home, and for six months, was the center of our attention. But suddenly, she was unable to keep food down. The doctor diagnosed her illness as a virus and prescribed penicillin. Three days later, she remained unchanged, and the doctor prescribed more penicillin. That night her condition became severe and we took her to Lutheran Hospital in Fort Wayne, Indiana. The pediatrician examined her and said her bowel was inverted and surgery was needed. He assured us that we would be able to take her home in three days.

After five hours of waiting, we inquired about her condition and were told she had been taken to another floor—and we could go to the fifth floor and use that waiting room. On arrival, two doctors met us and said Heather had suffered cardiac arrest and they were working on her. After 30 anxiety-filled minutes, the doctors returned to tell us that she had passed. We thought we were immune to this kind of loss—that it only happened to other families, not ours. "How could God be so cruel to take our baby?" I thought.

But the wealth of faith and fortitude my parents transferred to me would carry us through. We had been blessed with two other daughters, and after the third baby, Linda had a tubal ligation and pregnancy was not an option to continue growth in the family. God didn't answer all our questions, but He gave us peace and continued to strengthen and lead us. While I was the principal at a local school, we decided to add another child to our family. The school's social worker told me she would help us find a baby to adopt.

NEW ARRIVALS

Three months later, we were interviewing to adopt an 11-month-old boy named Michael. When the agency advised us that Michael had an older brother and sister, we said we would take all three and keep the family together, but the little girl's grandmother said she would keep the granddaughter. The social agency advised that the adoption procedure would require that we keep the boys for one year until the adoption process was finalized. The boys were a handful and we sometimes wondered if we had made the right decision. But we stuck with it, and the adoption was completed. Some of God's gifts take time to unwrap.

ANOTHER TRAGEDY

Raising children in *today's* world is challenging, to say the least. So, I am glad we can apply the ancient but always relevant wisdom of God's Word to family living. And what came next in our lives demanded every promised help in that Word. Both of our adopted sons had lingering effects from their original homelife, as is often the case. Prior to their adoption, we were told their mother claimed they both suffered from cerebral palsy or muscular dystrophy. After having the boys checked with a series of tests at the hospital and by a physician, we found her claim was not true. They didn't have either disease. We assumed she used the illnesses to justify or compensate for giving the boys up or to receive added benefits.

The youngest, Michael, joined the Marine Corp after his high school graduation as an infantry soldier and served two tours of duty in Iraq and Afghanistan. He was part of the company of American Marines who made the final push to liberate Baghdad. He was involved in Operation Iraqi Freedom, where his force liberated the town of Nasiriya and lost 18 men, the most from any US unit during the war. Like my dad, the war didn't end when Michael came home. He was diagnosed with PTSD.

One day I received a text message from him that simply said, "being stupid." This was not a normal message from Michael. A day earlier Linda and I had breakfast with him, and as we dropped him off afterward, he said the usual, "Love you, Mom and Dad." So, his "being stupid" text was alarming. I immediately thought he had been picked up for drinking since he had been drinking excessively on a regular basis. Although his mother and I never drank or brought alcohol into our home, Michael had acquired a taste for it while serving in the Marines. When I asked about the drinking, he said, "Dad, we generally worked from 8:00 a.m. to 5:00 p.m., and then drank beer until we went to bed at 10:00 p.m., night after night." Mike had attended Alcoholics Anonymous meetings in Marion but had not been regular in attending.

When I received the text, I was putting vinyl siding on my daughter and son-in-law's rental house. But I decided to quickly gather my tools and go to his house.

As I approached, I noticed his Jeep had been moved from its normal spot. The window on the front porch was open with only the screen down. Rushing to the window, I looked through the screen and yelled, "Michael! Michael!" There was no response, so I called the County Sheriff's office and the Marion Police Department to see if they had any word on him, and they hadn't. I returned home and waited for a call. Later that evening, the doorbell rang. I opened it to see two men with somber faces. They asked if they could talk with us. Linda was in the bedroom, so I called her. We sat in the living room, and I said, "I assume you have information on Mike?"

One of the men, the county coroner, said, "Yes. We're sorry to tell you, but it appears that Michael has taken his life." The other man, a sheriff's department chaplain, explained that Mike had backed his Jeep into the detached garage behind his house, closed the overhead door, and allowed the engine to run, resulting in his death. Three days later, our son was given a full military funeral and laid to rest in the Marion National Cemetery. Once again, our lives were changed beyond description.

Before losing Mike, I had interests in other organizations with my charitable dollars. And I had always made the point in my seminars that we should give to organizations that directly affect our families. But after this incident, our family developed a new interest in a project called Wreath's Across America that purchases wreaths for the Marion National Cemetery in Marion, Indiana. As of September 2018, there were 11,327 gravesites, and the goal is to lay a wreath on each grave. And when we lay wreaths on graves at that cemetery, we pause by Michael's gravesite and silently thank God for his life and his love. And we thank God for His grace that brought us through the pain of losing our children to the joy of teaching others the lessons He has taught us along the way. As a fundraiser, I am not the same after the loss of Michael. I have a new determination to raise monies for nonprofits that teach next generations how to deal with life issues in a practical and biblical way.

Terry Munday

ABOUT THE AUTHOR

Terry Munday has been called THE EXPERT on teaching the foundational principles of fundraising. He served 20 years as Vice-President for University Advancement at Indiana Wesleyan University in Marion, Indiana. During his two decades as its chief fund-raiser, IWU rose from the brink of bankruptcy to become one of America's fastest-growing Christian universities, with enrollment now exceeding 13,000 students. Munday, who has a master's and a specialist in education degrees, went from teaching and coaching to serving 14 years as a public school administrator, including eight years as a superintendent. While semi-retired from Indiana Wesleyan University, he continues to write and to serve as a consultant to IWU, his local church, and other Christian non-profit organizations. He has helped over 100 organizations raise more than $100 million. Terry's book, *It's Not About the Money* is a chronicle of his fundraising career and his Christian influence on both the well-known and the less-known. Munday also conducts fundraising seminars and speaks in institutions, conferences, and conventions across the nation.

Terry and his wife Linda, both Ohio natives, have been married for over 50 years and live in Marion, Indiana, to be near their three children and eight grandchildren.

Contact information:
Terry Munday
501 E. 48th Street
Marion, Indiana 46953
terry.munday@indwes.edu

NOTES

Chapter 1

1   David Kotter in *For the Least of These: A Biblical Answer to Poverty*, Anne R. Bradley (Nashville: Thomas Nelson, 2014), p. 57

2   https://wolfstreet.com/2018/04/17/nearly-one-third-of-u-s-lottery-winners-declare-bankruptcy/ (Accessed October 16, 2019

3   Greg Laurie, "What Did Jesus Teach About Wealth," https://www.christianity.com/jesus/life-of-jesus/teaching-and-messages/what-did-jesus-teach-about-wealth.html, (Accessed October 11, 2019).

4   Billy Smith and Larry ten Harmsel, *Fred Meijer: Stories of His Life*, (Grand Rapids: William B. Eerdmans Publishing Company, 2009), p. 282

5   Peter Singer, "What Should a Billionaire Give – and What Should You?"/ The New York Times July 13, 1019/https://www.nytimes.com/2006/12/17/magazine/17charity.t.html (Accessed December 15, 2019).

Chapter 2

6   Greg Laurie, "Money and Motives," www.oneplace.com/ministries/a-new-beginning/read/articles/money-and-motives-9220.html (Accessed October 8, 2019)

7   Ron Blue, *Master Your Money*, (Chicago: Moody Publishers, 2016), p. 8

8   Willaim A. Dembski, "The Act of Creation: Bridging Transcendence and Immanence,"/http://www.arn.org/docs/dembski/wd_actofcreation.htm, (Accessed October 19, 2019).

9   "Jewish Laws for Inheritance," https://bibleask.org/what-are-some-of-the-jewish-laws-for-inheritance-according-to-the-old-testament (Accessed October 8, 2019).

10   Ron Blue, Master Your Money / (Chicago: Moody Publishers, 2016), p. 8

11   "Reasons for the Year of Jubilee," Smiths Bible Dictionary / https://biblehub.com/topical/t/the_year_of_jubilee.htm

12   Caitlin Burke, "Churches Join the Hottest New Business Trend: The 'Sharing Economy'"/ CBN News, December 17, 2019 / https://www1.cbn.com/cbnnews/us/2019/december/churches-join-the-hottest-new-business-trend-the-sharing-economy (Accessed December 17, 2019).

13   Gordon MacDonald, *Generosity: Moving Toward Life That Is Truly Life*, (Generous Church, 2013), p. 9

14   "Holy Ground," words and music by Geron Davis, copyright 1983 by Meadowgreen Music Company/Songchannel

Chapter 3

15   Lee J. Colan, "What are You Leaving Behind—An Inheritance or a Legacy?" / *Adviser FP*, August 27, 2018 / https://www.adviserfp.com.au/what-are-you-leaving-behind-an-inheritance-or-a-legacy/ (Accessed December 14, 2019).

16   Blair Shiff, "Charles Schwab: If you start investing at this age, you're making a mistake" / *Business Leaders*, October 14, 2019 / https://www.foxbusiness.com/business-leaders/charles-schwab-advice-new-investors

17   Roger Bannister, https://en.wikipedia.org/wiki/Roger_Bannister, (Accessed October 11, 2019).

18   John Tucker, "You Take This House, and I'll Take Yours" / *The Chicken*

Wire, November 1, 2019 / https://thechickenwire.chick-fil-a.com/ Inside-Chick-fil-A/You-take-this-house-and-Ill-take-yours (Accessed December 14, 2019).

Chapter 4

19   Tim Cestnick, "Distributing Your Estate to Your Heirs," The Globe and Mail, https://www.theglobeandmail.com/globe-investor/personal -finance/taxes/distributing-your-estate-to-your-heirs-the-methods- and-the-message/article19641684/, (Accessed October 18, 2019).

20   John J. Havens and Paul G. Schervish/ "A Golden Age of Philanthropy Still Beckons: National Wealth Transfer and Potential for Philanthropy Technical Report"/ Boston College Center on Wealth and philanthropy/ https://www.bc.edu/content/dam/files/research_ sites/cwp/pdf/A%20Golden%20Age%20of%20Philanthropy%20 Still%20Bekons.pdf (Accessed October 24, 2019)

21   https://www.cnbc.com/2014/05/28/greatest-wealth-transfer- in-history-underway-59-trillion-to-heirs-charity-by-2061.html (Accessed October 24, 2019).

22   Ibid.

23   Availablehttps://finance.yahoo.com/news/family-conflict-reigns-great est-threat-131800794.html? (Accessed December 21, 2019).

24   Diana Arneson, "What are some pros and cons of the baby boomer generation?"/ *Quora*, November 10, 2019 / https://www.quora. com/What-are-some-pros-and-cons-of-the-baby-boomer-generation (Accessed December 30, 2019).

25   Mackenzie Sigalos, "$68 trillion is about to change hands in the US,"/ CNBC November 20, 2018/ https://www.cnbc.com/2018/11/20/ great-wealth-transfer-is-passing-from-baby-boomers-to-gen-x- millennials.html

26 https://www.macrotrends.net/countries/USA/united-states/life-expectancy (Accessed October 25, 2019)

27 David Spiegelhalter, "Life expectancy: How long will you live?"/BBC April 9, 2012 (Accessed October 25, 2019)

28 Paul G. Schervish/ "A Golden Age of Philanthropy Still Beckons: National Wealth Transfer and Potential for Philanthropy Technical Report"

29 Christian E. Weller, Connor Maxwell, and Danyelle Solomon, "Simulating How Progressive Proposals Affect the Racial Wealth Gap", Center for American Progress, August 7, 2019/ https://www.americanprogress.org/issues/race/reports/2019/08/07/473117/simulating-progressive-proposals-affect-racial-wealth-gap/ (Accessed October 25, 2019)

30 Tony Martignetti , "Beyond Bequests: Common Planned Gifts That Don't Require In-House Expertise" / *NonProfitPro,* December 18, 2019 / https://www.nonprofitpro.com / (Accessed December 30, 2019).

31 Source Unknown

32 https://ropercenter.cornell.edu/featured-collections/2006-social-capital-community-benchmark-survey (Accessed October 26, 2019)

33 Bamidele Onibalusi, "Billionaires' Secret: Is Giving the Key to Wealth?", Effective Business Ideas/ https://www.effectivebusinessideas.com/giving-and-wealth/ (Accessed October 18, 2019)

34 Tim Chestnick.

35 https://www.privatebank.bankofamerica.com/articles/2018-us-trust-study-of-high-net-worth-philanthropy.html

Chapter 5

36   https://givingusa.org/giving-usa-2019-americans-gave-427-71-billion-to-charity-in-2018-amid-complex-year-for-charitable-giving/ (Accessed October 27, 2019)

37   Staff written, "An Intro to Generations" / The Center for Generational Kinetics / https://genhq.com/FAQ-info-about-generations/ (Accessed November 1, 2019).

38   The Greatest Generation / Wikipedia / https://en.wikipedia.org/wiki/Greatest_Generation (Accessed December 25, 2019).

39   Patrict Kiger, "Boomer Generation is the Most Charitable, Study Finds" / *AARP.org* May 7, 2018 / https://www.aarp.org/money/budgeting-saving/info-2018/boomers-most-charitable.html (Accessed November 2, 2019).

40   Staff written, "Listening for the Silent Generation"/ Sharpe Group / https://sharpenet.com/give-take/listening-for-the-silent-generation/ (Accessed November 2, 2019).

41   U. S. News & World Report, 2015 Baby Boomer Report / https://www.usnews.com/pubfiles/USNews_Market_Insights_Boomers2015.pdf

42   Adam Vaccaro, "Young Talent: What to Expect From the Post-Millennial Workforce" / https://www.inc.com/adam-vaccaro/generation-after-millennials.html (Accessed October 21, 2109)

43   Richard Fry "Gen X rebounds as the only generation to recover the wealth lost after the housing crash" / Pew Research Center Fact Tank / July 23, 2018 / https://www.pewresearch.org/fact-tank/2018/07/23/gen-x-rebounds-as-the-only-generation-to-recover-the-wealth-lost-after-the-housing-crash/ (Accessed October 28, 2019)

44 Jean M. Twenge, "Millennials: The Greatest Generation or the Most Narcissistic?"/The Atlantic May 2, 2012/ https://www.theatlantic.com/national/archive/2012/05/millennials-the-greatest-generation-or-the-most-narcissistic/256638/ (Accessed November 2, 2019).

45 Staff written, "An Intro to Generations" / The Center for Generational Kinetics / https://genhq.com/FAQ-info-about-generations/ (Accessed November 1, 2019).

46 Anne Gherini, "Gen-Z Is About to Outnumber Millennials. Here's How That Will Affect the Business World"/ Inc.Aug 22, 2018 (Accessed November 1, 2019).

47 Alice Berg, "Who is Generation Z?" / Classy.org / https://www.classy.org/blog/gen-z-next-generation-donors/ (Accessed November 1, 2019).

48 "Generation Z" / Wikipedia / https://en.wikipedia.org/wiki/Generation_Z / (Accessed November 1, 2019).

49 Ibid.

50 Ibid.

51 Amay Anatole, "Generation Z: Rebels With A Cause", / *Forbes* on Marketing May 28, 2013 / https://www.forbes.com/sites/onmarketing/2013/05/28/generation-z-rebels-with-a-cause/#12b9805269c2 (Accessed November 1, 2019).

52 George Barna, *America at the Crossroads: Explosive Trends Shaping America's Future and What You Can Do about It* / (Grand Rapids: Baker Books 2016), P. 129

Chapter 6

53 Patricia Snell Herzog and Heather E. Price, *American Generosity: Who Gives and Why* / (New York: Oxford University Press 2016) p. 172

54 "DAF: 5 Ways Philanthropists Use Donor Advised Funds and How Fundraisers Can Benefit" / NPT and DonorPerfect / https://uploads.donorperfect.com/pdf/daf.pdf (Accessed December 31, 2019).

55 Crawford Heritage Community Foundation / Available online: https://www.crawfordheritage.org/wp-content/uploads/2019/10/samplebequestattys.pdf

56 Thomas Hlubin, "Fear of Poverty" / Psychtimes.com / https://psychtimes.com/peniaphobia-fear-of-poverty (Accessed November 9, 2019)

57 Becky Kleanthous, "How Much is a Trillion" / The Calculator Site August 3, 2018 / https://www.thecalculatorsite.com/articles/finance/how-much-is-a-trillion.php (Accessed November 6, 2019)

58 Claire Axelrad, "Loyalty vs. Capacity: Distinguishing Between Planned and Major Gift Prospects" / *Bloomerang* November 11, 2019 /https://bloomerang.co/blog/loyalty-vs-capacity-distinguishing-between-planned-and-major-gift-prospects/ (Accessed December 31, 2019).

59 Ibid.

60 J. Chucks, "Population Ageing in Ghana: Research Gaps and the Way Forward"/ *Journal of Aging Research* 2010/ https://www.hindawi.com/journals/jar/2010/672157/ (Accessed October 29, 2019)

Chapter 7

61 J. Walker Smith and Ann Clurman, Preface. *Rocking the Ages: The Yankelovich Report on Generational Marketing* / (New York: Harper Collins 1997), p. XVII

62 Jenna Spinelle, "A Breakdown of Millennial Debt & What the Numbers Look Like Now" / Credit Sesame June 2016 / https://www.

creditsesame.com/blog/debt/breakdown-millennial-debt/ (Accessed November 13, 2019).

63 *Giving USA* Foundation Press release / http://www.givingusa.org/press_releases/gusa.cfm

64 George Barna, *America at the Crossroads*, p. 27

Chapter 8

65 David Noland and Barbara Peterson, "12 Plane Crashes That Changed Aviation" / *Popular Mechanics*, August 4, 2017 / https://www.popularmechanics.com/flight/g73/12-airplane-crashes-that-changed-aviation/ (Accessed December 31, 2019).

66 Jerold Panas, "The 5 Factors to Ensure Your Amazing Success" / *Jerold Panas, Linzy & Partners, LLC* / https://panaslinzy.com/wp-content/uploads/2019/11/the-5-factors-to-ensure-your-amazing (Accessed November 27, 2019).

67 Janet Levinger, "Fundraising and Values"/*LeadingWell.org. October 16, 2019 / https://leadingwell.org/2019/10/16/fundraising-and-values/* (Accessed November 28, 2019).

68 Amy Eisenstein, "How Big is a Major Gift" / *Amy Eisenstein: Empowering Your Nonprofit—and You* / https://www.amyeisenstein.com/how-big-is-a-major-gift/ (Accessed December 1, 2019).

69 Jerold Panas, "The 5 Factors to Ensure Your Amazing Success"

70 Jeff Reeves, "Plan Ahead: 64% of Americans don't have a will" / Usa Today July 11, 2015 / https://www.usatoday.com/story/money/personalfinance/2015/07/11/estate-plan-will/71270548/ (Accessed December 2, 2019).

72 Stephan M. Pollan and Mark Levine, *Die Broke* (New York: HarperCollins 1997 by Stephan M. Pollan and Mark Levine), p. 297

73 "Planned Gift Varieties" / *Donorsearch* / https://www.donorsearch. net/planned-gifts-complete-guide/ (Accessed December 4, 2019).

74 Stephan M. Pollan and Mark Levine, *Die Broke,* p. 115

75 Julia Kagan, "Charitable Remainder Trust" / *Investopedia* June 27, 2019 /https://www.investopedia.com/terms/c/charitableremaindertrust.asp /c/charitableremaindertrust.asp (Accessed December 4, 2019).

76 "What to Know About Gifting Stocks" / *Edward Jones – Making Sense of Investing / https://www.edwardjones.com/social/gifted-stock.html jones. com/social/gifted-stock.html (Accessed December 4, 2019).*

77 Kimberly Lankford, "5 Things You Should Know About Giving Stock to Charity" / Kiplinger, December 1, 2015 / https://www.kiplinger. com/article/taxes/T054-C001-S001-giving-stock-to-charity.html (Accessed December 5, 2019).

78 Robin Cabral/ "Putting More Thought into the Direct Mail Reply Envelope"/ *NonProfitPRO*, November 21, 2019 / nonprofitpro.com (Accessed December 31, 2019).

Chapter 9

79 Shainna Ali, "What Your Need to Know About the Loneliness Epidemic" / *Psychology Today,* July 12, 2018 / https://www. psychologytoday.com/us/blog/modern-mentality/201807/what-you-need-know-about-the-loneliness-epidemic (Accessed December 8, 2019).

80 John Edmond Haggai, *Paul J. Meyer and the Art of Giving*, (Tulsa: Insight Publishing Group, Copyright 1994 by John Edmond Haggai), p. 49

81 Ann Green "Show Your Donors How Much You Care About Them" / *Ann Green's Nonprofit Blog*, April 25, 2018 / https://anngreennonprofit.

com/2018/04/25/show-your-donors-how-much-you-care-about-them (Accessed December 8, 2019).

82 Johnathon Grapsas, "Brilliant donor care: 15 steps to make sure your organization gets it right" / *Sofii.org*, January 15, 2013 / http://sofii. org/article/fifteen-steps-to-brilliant-donor-care-how-to-make-sure-your-organisation-gets-it-right (Accessed December 9, 2019).

83 John Edmond Haggai, *Paul J. Meyer and the Art of Giving*, p. 80

84 David Green, *More than a Hobby*, p. 40-41.

85 Claire Axelrad, "Top Ten Ways to Say 'Thank You!' to Donors" / *Bloomerang, February 6, 2018* / https://bloomerang.co/blog/top-10-ways-to-say-thank-you-to-donors/ (Accessed December 9, 2019).

86 Smith and Clurman, *Rocking the Ages*, p. 288

Chapter 10

87 Jenna Goudreau, "A Harvard Psychologist Says People Judge You Based on 2 Criteria When They First Meet You" / Harvard *Business Insider*-Australia, December 29, 2016 / https://www.businessinsider.com.au/harvard-psychologist-amy-cuddy-how-people-judge-you-2016-1 (Accessed December 12, 2019).

88 Michael Stelzner / "Neuroscience and Marketing: How People Make Decisions"/ *Social Media Examiner*, December 20, 2019 / https://www.socialmediaexaminer.com/neuroscience-marketing-how-people-make-decisions-tracy-trost/ (Accessed December 29, 2019).

89 Mother Teresa / *AZ Quotes* / https://www.azquotes.com/author/14530-Mother_Teresa (Accessed January 8, 2020).